LONG-TERM LEASING—
ACCOUNTING, EVALUATION,
CONSEQUENCES

LONG-TERM LEASING— ACCOUNTING, EVALUATION, CONSEQUENCES

Ahmed Riahi-Belkaoui

Q

QUORUM BOOKS
Westport, Connecticut • London

Library of Congress Cataloging-in-Publication Data

Riahi-Belkaoui, Ahmed, 1943–
    Long-term leasing—accounting, evaluation, consequences / Ahmed
Riahi-Belkaoui.
        p.   cm.
    Includes bibliographical references and index.
    ISBN 1–56720–147–4 (alk. paper)
    1. Leases—Accounting. 2. Lease or buy decisions. I. Title.
    HF5681.L3R53   1998
    657'.75—dc21   97–22749

British Library Cataloguing in Publication Data is available.

Library of Congress Catalog Card Number: 97–22749
ISBN: 1–56720–147–4

First published in 1998

Quorum Books, 88 Post Road West, Westport, CT 06881
An imprint of Greenwood Publishing Group, Inc.

Printed in the United States of America

The paper used in this book complies with the
Permanent Paper Standard issued by the National
Information Standards Organization (Z39.48–1984).

10 9 8 7 6 5 4 3 2 1

Copyright Acknowledgment

FASB Statement No. 13, *Accounting for Leases*, is copyrighted by the Financial Accounting Standards Board, 401 Merritt 7, P.O. Box 5116, Norwalk, CT 06856-5116, U.S.A. Portions are reprinted
with permission. Complete copies of this document are available from the FASB.

To My Family

Contents

Exhibits   ix

Preface and Acknowledgments   xi

1. Analysis of the Lease-or-Buy Decision   1

2. Accounting for Long-Term Leases: Part I   39

3. Accounting for Long-Term Leases: Part II   53

4. Issues in Accounting for Long-Term Leases   81

5. The Economics of Buying   99

Index   143

Exhibits

1.1.	Approaches to Lease Evaluation	16
1.2.	Decision Format Table	24
1.3.	Decision Format Graph	25
2.1.	Alvertos Company: Lease Amortization Schedule (Annuity Due Basis)	44
2.2.	Alvertos Company: Changes to Operations—Capital Lease Versus Operating Lease	46
2.3.	Zribi Company: Lease Amortization Schedule (Annuity Due Basis)	50
3.1.	Zribi's Computation of Lease Payments in the Case of Residual Value (Lessor's Computation, Annuity Due Basis)	54
3.2.	Alvertos Company Lease Amortization Schedule (Lessee's Computation, Annuity Due Basis) and Guaranteed Residual Value (GRV)	55
3.3.	Alvertos Company Lease Amortization Schedule (Lessee's Computation, Annuity Due Basis) and Unguaranteed Residual Value	57
3.4.	Zribi Company Lease Amortization Schedule (Lessor's Computation, Annuity Due Basis) and Guaranteed Residual Value	59
3.5.	Lessee's Lease Amortization Schedule	64

3.6.   Cash Flow Analysis by Years   70

3.7.   Allocation of Annual Cash Flow to Investment and Income   71

3.8.   Allocation of Annual Cash Flow to Investment and Income, Revised to Include New Residual Value Estimate   75

3.9.   Balances in Investment Accounts Before Revised Estimate of Residual Value   76

3.10. Adjustment of Investment Accounts for Revised Estimates of Residual Value in the Eleventh Year   77

4.1.   McDonald's Corporation Financial Statement Data and Leasing Footnote   85

4.2.   McDonald's Operating Leases: Equivalent Present Value   86

4.3.   Constructive Capitalization of Operating Leases: Relation Between Unrecorded Liability and Unrecorded Asset Over Time   87

4.4.   Impact of Constructive Capitalization of Operating Leases on McDonald's Balance Sheet and Financial Ratios   88

4.5.   Impact of Constructive Capitalization of Operating Leases on Seven Industry Pairings   89

5.1.   Reconciliation of Cash Flow and Accounting Income   102

5.2.   Amortization Schedule: Proof for the Internal Rate of Return   106

5.3.   Amortization Schedule Underlying the Net Present Value   110

5.4.   Relationship Between Net Present Value and Internal Rate of Return   113

5.5.   Mutually Exclusive Investments: Scale Effects   114

5.6.   Mutually Exclusive Investments: Timing Effects   115

5.7.   Mutually Exclusive Investments: Different Lives   116

5.8.   Replacement Decision Analysis   123

5.9.   Capital Rationing Example   126

5.10. Decision Tree Approach to Capital Budgeting   135

Preface and Acknowledgments

Leasing is by far the most important source of finance for various types of assets needed by firms. Problems that may arise are either in the decision to buy or lease, or the accounting decision to capitalize or expense. This book addresses both problems by examining the models and standards used for both management and accounting for leases. The main purpose of this book is to present the models and standards that may be useful to decision makers, financial accountants, and researchers interested in management and accounting for leases.

The book consists of five chapters. Chapter 1 covers the issues involved in the lease-financing decision models and offers a decision format to reconcile the disagreements among the various approaches to the lease-or-buy analysis. Chapters 2 and 3 cover all the techniques proposed for accounting for long-term leases as formulated by Statement of Accounting Standards No. 13. Chapter 4 covers the issues involved in accounting for long-term leases. Chapter 5 covers the economics of buying.

Many people helped in the development of this book. Considerable assistance was received from the University of Illinois at Chicago students, especially Dimitra K. Alvertos and Saras Natarajan. I also thank Eric Valentine and the entire production team at Greenwood Publishing for their contributions and intelligent support. Finally, to Hedi and Janice thanks for making life so exciting.

1

Analysis of the Lease-or-Buy Decision

Leasing has recently become an important source of financing for many types of assets. The lessee acquires the use of an asset while the title is retained by the lessor. More specifically, a lease is a contract between an owner (the lessor) and another party (the lessee) that grants the lessee the right to use the lessor's property under certain conditions and for a specified period of time. Because of the contractual nature of lease obligation, a lease should be considered a financing device and an alternative to debt financing. Both the lease rental payments and the payments of principal and interest on debt are fixed obligations. Any default in the payment of either obligation can create serious problems.

The decision to lease an asset is generally evaluated by comparing it with a borrowing decision necessary for an outright purchase of the same asset; different valuation models have been proposed, and any choice can be challenged because of the controversial issues surrounding a given model and its corresponding variables and parameters. The main purpose of this chapter is to explain leasing arrangements and the main issues in financial leasing, and to provide a methodology for analysis.

The lease as a new form of financing undergoes constant change, as shown by the number and variations of the sources of leasing arrangements. Financial institutions involved in leasing differ mainly in their degree of specialization and include independent leasing companies, service leasing companies, lease brokers, commercial brokers, and insurance companies.

TYPES OF LEASING ARRANGEMENTS

Although it is possible to describe major forms of lease arrangements, the options, terms, and conditions may vary from contract to contract, giving a firm great flexibility in the adaptation of leasing as a financing method.

Operating versus Financial Leases

The first distinction to be made in leasing is between *operating and financial leases*. Under both contracts, the lessee agrees to make periodic rental payments. An operating lease is a short-term contract that is cancelable given proper notice at the option of the lessee, whereby the lessor gives the lessee the use of property in exchange for rental payments and at the same time retains the usual ownership risks (such as obsolescence) and rewards (such as a gain from appreciation in value at the end of the lease period). To compensate the lessor for assuming the ownership risks, the periodic rental payments of an operating lease will include a return on investment plus most ownership costs, such as maintenance, taxes, depreciation, obsolescence, casualty losses, and so forth. Examples of operating leases include car rentals, apartment rentals, telephone service, and space rental in shopping centers.

A financial lease is a comparatively long-term contract that is non-cancelable by the lessor, who assumes little or no ownership costs. As a result, the periodic rental payments include only a return on investment, and the lessee may be required to pay most of the ownership costs. At the termination of the lease, options may exist allowing the lessee to acquire the asset at either a nominal cost or no cost at all. The financial lease allows the lessor to recover the investment and even realize a profit through the lessee's continuous rental payments over the period specified by the contract. The financial lease gives the lessee continuous use of the asset at a certain cost and, consequently, is a means of financing the use (but not the ownership) of the asset. In other words, the difference between the operating and financial lease lies mainly in the cancellation and financing options. As opposed to an operating lease, a financial lease is noncancelable, and it can be perceived as a financing instrument.

Sale and Leaseback, Direct Leasing, and Leverage Leases

Another important distinction in lease financing is made between the sale and leaseback and direct lease arrangements. The difference lies in the nature of the prior ownership of the asset to be leased. Under the sale and leaseback arrangement, a firm sells an asset it owns to another party, which in turn leases it back to the previous owner. Under this popular arrangement, a company in need of liquidity receives cash from the sale of the asset while retaining the economic use of the asset during the lease period.

Under direct leasing, the lessee acquires the use of an asset it did not previously own. The lessee can enter into the leasing arrangements with a manufacturer, independent leasing company, or financial institution.

With the advent of direct leasing through commercial banks in 1963, a new lease arrangement appeared, called a leverage lease. This is a tripartite arrangement whereby the lessor finances a portion of the acquisition of the asset (50 to 80 percent of the purchase price) from a lender (commercial bank), securing the loan by a mortgage of the leased property as well as by the assignment of the lease and lease payments. The leverage lease is a popular instrument for special-purpose leasing companies and partnerships of individuals in high tax brackets because of the tax benefits provided by the accelerated depreciation charges, the investment tax credit, the interest on debt, and the favorable return on the equity participation by the lessor. From the point of view of the lessee, the leverage lease is similar to any other lease and, consequently, does not affect the method of valuation.[1]

Leverage leasing involves at least four parties: a lessee, a manufacturer (or distributor), a lessor, and a lender. Arrangements are complex, and the parties enter into the agreement primarily for tax and financial cost savings rather than convenience. The lessee is able to obtain financial leasing from the lessor at a cost lower than the usual cost of capital; the lessor, being of a high income tax bracket, gains an investment tax credit (or capital cost allowance) benefit resulting in reduced taxes. The lessor passes on some of this benefit to the lessee through reduced lease costs. Direct leasing, sale and leaseback, and leverage leasing are illustrated later in Exhibit 1.1

Maintenance, Nonmaintenance, and Net Leases

The assignment of responsibility for the maintenance of the asset during the life of a lease takes three forms: maintenance lease, nonmaintenance lease, and net lease.

A *maintenance lease* assigns responsibility for the maintenance of a leased asset's good working order to the lessor. The lessor is required to incur the maintenance and repair expenses and the local and state taxes, and to provide insurance for the leased asset. The maintenance lease is preferable when the lessor is better equipped to provide low-cost repair than the lessee in terms of technology and skills. It is used mostly in rentals of automobiles, trucks, and specialized equipment, like computers, requiring a highly qualified maintenance staff.

A *nonmaintenance lease* assigns the responsibility for the maintenance of a leased asset to the lessee. The lessee is required to pay for all maintenance and repair costs and the local and state taxes, and to provide insurance. The nonmaintenance lease occurs principally in long-term leasing of land and buildings.

A *net lease* assigns total responsibility for an asset's maintenance to the lessee to the point that the lessee may be required to absorb all losses incurred by the sale of the asset at the end of the life of the lease, which is typical in fleet leasing of vehicles. In car leasing the net lease is sometimes referred to as an open-end lease: In return for a slightly lower monthly lease fee, the lessee agrees to make up the price differential if the leased car sells for less than the prearranged price when the lease expires because of excess mileage, poor maintenance, or any other reason.

ADVANTAGES OF LEASING

Shifting the Risks of Ownership

A firm that purchases an asset is subject to the risk of obsolescence due to innovation in the field. Generally, in the decision to lease or buy an asset subject to a high rate of obsolescence, the leasing alternative will appear more appropriate. Through leasing rather than buying the asset, the lessee can shift the risk of obsolescence and of ownership to the lessor.

The argument in favor of leasing relies heavily on the assumption that the lessor is not aware of the rate of obsolescence and innovation in the field. In most cases, however, the lessor is very knowledgeable and is in a better position to anticipate the rate of obsolescence than the lessee. The lessor, well aware of the risks of ownership, will attempt to recover the investment plus interest over the lease period and will probably include an implicit charge for obsolescence in the computation of the rental payments. Only when the lessor inaccurately estimates the rate of obsolescence does the lessee benefit from shifting the risks of ownership. If the asset becomes obsolete more rapidly than the lessor anticipated, the leasing alternative will be beneficial to the lessee. The lessor can keep the rental payments low by spreading the risk of obsolescence over many lease contracts. The diversification in this case will benefit both the lessor and the lessee.

Avoidance of Restrictions Associated with Debt

Leasing is assumed to offer fewer restrictions than debt and, consequently, to provide more flexibility. Most loan agreements and bond indentures include protective covenant restrictions, but similar limitations are not as common in leasing. One usual restriction accompanying leasing is in the use of the leased property. For example, the use of the leased equipment may be limited in terms of the number of hours per day. Changes and adjustments in the lease equipment may also be prohibited unless authorized by the lessor.

The advantage of fewer restrictions with leasing than with debt financing will probably disappear in the near future. Most lenders impose restrictions on the amount to be leased for firms financed heavily by debt. Because leasing is becoming more and more accepted as a form of financing, protective covenants will probably be drafted for both leasing and bond indentures.

Effect on Cash Borrowing Capacity

It is often said that leasing allows a firm to conserve cash and raise more funds than debt financing. This is based on the following claims— some supportable and some unsupportable—made on behalf of leasing.

People often argue that leasing allows the optimal use of cash leading to an improvement in a firm's total earning power. Thus, it is maintained, the capital intended for the purchase of fixed assets with low turnover is tied up for the acquisition of current assets with high turnover. Retailers most often are advised to rent their premises and allocate their capital to inventory and accounts receivable. Although seemingly attractive, this claim on behalf of leasing is the result of confusion about the relationship between the investment and financing decisions. It assumes that the financing method is a determinant of the mix of assets. A firm actually decides first on the optimal mix of assets necessary for its line of business and then decides on the proper way of financing this mix by comparing the costs of buying and leasing. The firm can decide either to borrow or lease. In either case it decides to use the optimal mix of assets effectively and efficiently.

People also argue that leasing permits a firm not only to avoid buying an asset, but also to finance up to 100 percent of the cost of the asset. What is the impact on a firm's borrowing capacity? Does leasing provide more funds? The usual assumption is that leasing has no effect on a firm's borrowing power and a positive effect on its borrowing capacity. However, this line of reasoning is misleading. Given the fixed obligatory nature of the lease, it should be considered equivalent to an implicit loan of 100 percent of the funds needed. The borrowing capacity is definitely reduced, and the borrowing power must be compared with debt financing. The erroneous assumption that leasing provides more funds results from the conventional accounting treatment, whereby lease obligations are not shown by liabilities on the balance sheet. This situation has changed, and accounting treatments now tend to favor the capitalization of long-term leases.

Leasing permits the financing of capital additions on a piecemeal basis. To be practical, long-term debt financing must usually be arranged on a much larger scale than lease financing, which can be adjusted to each individual unit of property acquired. This can be a valid reason for using lease financing to make occasional asset acquisitions spaced over a period of time. However, this justification lost its validity when the total amount of capital additions over a given period is large enough to justify a debt issue. Long-term debt financing can be adapted to the timing of expenditures, either through the use of interim bank borrowings with subsequent refunding or by a direct placement of securities with institutional investors, providing for a series of takedowns.[2]

Tax Advantages

A common argument in the lease-or-buy controversy is whether leasing offers tax advantages over ownership. Under present tax laws, rental payments are considered an operating expense and can be deducted from taxable income. This gives rise to two basic differences in the tax effects of leasing as compared with ownership:

1. Leasing makes it possible, in effect, to write off the depreciable portion of property over the basic term of a lease, which is generally shorter than the period that would be permitted for depreciation. The result is not a tax savings but a shift in the timing of deductions and tax payments similar to the effects of accelerated depreciation. To the extent that tax payments are deferred, the company benefits by having the use of these funds for the additional period.

2. Leasing makes it possible, in effect, to write off land value against taxable income, which is not allowed for depreciation purposes. The effect can be very significant when land represents a substantial portion of the total investments in urban department store properties. Although leasing provides a way to recover part of the investment in land during the basic periods of the lease, it also deprives the company of 100 percent of this value at the end of the period—which still leaves a net loss of 48 percent. Furthermore, if past trends in land value are any indication of future trends, the loss could be considerably greater.[3]

Another cost implicitly packaged in the terms of any leasing contract is corrected with the federal income tax deduction. One of the frequently cited advantages of equipment leasing is that a leasing contract permits the lessee to enjoy a more advantageous stream of income tax expense deductions than would be possible with outright ownership of the equipment, where only depreciation and interest could be deducted. In fact, there may be some advantage if the lease payments are scheduled so they are higher in the earlier years of the lease than the sum of depreciation and interest and, conversely, lower in later years. Under these conditions, the present value of the tax deductions is greater than under outright ownership. This advantage can be achieved in another way under financial leases. The agreement can be made for a relatively short initial term—say five years. During this time the lessor recovers the entire cost of the equipment: If the lessee purchased the equipment directly, it would have to be depreciated over a longer time span—say, seven to ten years.[4]

The Economic Recovery Tax Act of 1981 allows companies to transfer the tax benefits of tax credits and of the Accelerated Cost Recovery System (ACRS) on new plants and equipment bought between January 1 and August 13, 1981, through what is called safe-harbor leasing. Such transactions are safe as long as the letter of the Internal Revenue Service regulations is followed. This is possible in two cases:

1. Under a reciprocal lease-sublease, the seller of the tax benefits (the

lessor-sublessee) acquires new equipment for its own use and, within three months of purchase, leases it to the buyer of the tax credits (the lessee-sublessor). The seller transfers tax credits to the buyer via the lease, and the buyer simultaneously subleases the property back to the seller (the user) without those credits. The rentals payable by the buyer exceed the rentals to be received by the buyer. This differential is effectively the purchase price of the tax credits transferred.

2. Under a sale leaseback, the seller of the tax benefits (the seller and lessee of the property) acquires new equipment for its own use and, within three months of purchase, sells it to the buyer of the tax benefits (the buyer and lessor of the property). This enables the seller to transfer to the buyer the tax benefits related to the equipment. The consideration is composed of a cash down payment of at least 10 percent of the original cost of the property and a note for the remainder. The buyer then leases the property back to the seller for a lease term that is equal to the term of the note. If the rentals under the lease are equal to the payments on the note (principal and interest), the buyer's initial investment (the down payment) is the purchase price of the tax benefits. The seller continues to be the user of the property. The seller may retain title to the property or reacquire title at the end of the lease term for a nominal amount, such as $1.[5]

The intent of the legislation is that tax leases will allow firms that do not owe taxes or are unable to realize certain tax benefits to realize those benefits by making them transferable. Instead of receiving the benefits directly as a reduction of income taxes payable, firms not owing taxes can realize them by selling the right to those benefits to other firms that can use them to reduce taxes payable.

Shortly after the passage of the act, Ford Motor Company announced that it was selling to International Business Machines Corporation (IBM) its investment tax and depreciation deductions on "under $1 billion" worth of machinery, equipment, and tools acquired so far in 1981. Similarly, Bethlehem Steel Corp. and R. R. Donnelley & Sons Co. entered into a safe-harbor lease transaction that involves the exchange of tax credits. Donnelley will buy steel manufacturing equipment from Bethlehem and lease it back to the steel maker.

A NORMATIVE MODEL FOR LEASE EVALUATION

Any model for lease evaluation is determined on a cash flow basis. The treatment of the variable in the model differs, depending on whether it is the lessee's or the lessor's model.

Lessor's Analysis

The lessor attempts to determine a rental payment amount that will insure that the present value of rental payments plus the present value of the salvage value of the asset equals or exceeds the original cost of the asset. The discount rate the lessor chooses will be adjusted for the recovery of both the cost of capital of the lessor and other ownership costs before taxes. The lessee may have the option of paying the rental payments at the beginning or the end of each year. Both cases will be examined using the following sample problem.

Assume a firm has decided to lease an asset under the following conditions:

Purchase price of the asset $(A_o) = \$30,000$

Expected salvage value of the asset $(S) = \$10,000$

Before-tax rate of return $(K_1) = 8$ percent

Salvage value discount rate $(K_s) = 20$ percent

Lease period (n) = 5 years.

To compute the rental payment, proceed as follows:
1. The present value of the salvage value (Spv) is

$$S_{PV} = \frac{S}{(1 + K_s)^n} = \frac{\$10,000}{(1 + 0.20)^5} = \$4,018.$$

2. The rental (R_j) if paid in advance is

$$A_0 - S_{PV} = R_1 + \sum_{j=2}^{5} \frac{R_j}{(1 + K_L)^{j-1}}$$

$$= R_1 + \sum_{j=2}^{5} \frac{R_j}{(1 + 0.08)^{j-1}}$$

$$\$30,000 - \$4,018 = R_j(1 + 3.31213)$$

$$R_j = \$6,025$$

3. The rental (R_j) if paid at the end of period is

$$A_0 - S_{pv} = \sum_{j=1}^{n} R_j \frac{1}{(1 + K_L)^j}$$

$$\$30,000 - \$4,018 = \sum_{j=1}^{5} R_j \frac{1}{(1 + 0.08)^j}$$

$$= R_j \, (3.99271)$$

$$R_j = \$6,507$$

Lessee's Analysis

The lessee's approach concentrates on how the asset is to be acquired, leaving to more conventional capital budgeting techniques the prior decision on whether the asset is to be acquired at all. Thus, the question the lessee examines is whether to borrow and buy or to lease. The answer is found by comparing the respective costs of both alternatives. The summary measure used for the comparison can be either the net present value advantage of leasing (*NAL*) or the pretax interest rate on the lease (X_i). The *NAL* measure is expressed as follows:

$$NAL = A_0 - \underbrace{\sum_{j=1}^{n} \frac{R_j}{(1 + X_1)^j}}_{[1] \quad [2]} + \underbrace{\sum_{j=1}^{n} \frac{TR_j}{(1 + X_2)^j}}_{[3]} - \underbrace{\sum_{j=1}^{n} \frac{TD_j}{(1 + X_3)^j}}_{[4]} - \underbrace{\sum_{j=1}^{n} \frac{TI_j}{(1 + X_4)^j}}_{[5]}$$

$$+ \underbrace{\sum_{j=1}^{n} \frac{O_j(1 - T)}{(1 + X_5)^j}}_{[6]} - \underbrace{\frac{V_n}{(1 + K_s)^j}}_{[7]}$$

The variables included in the *NAL* equation are defined as follows:

A_o = Purchase price of the asset

R_j = Lease payment in period j

D_j = Depreciation charge in period j

V_n = Expected after-tax salvage value of the asset = $S_j - (S_j - B_j)\, T_g$

S_j = Salvage value in period j

B_j = Book value in period j

X_i = Discount rates to apply to the various cash flow streams of the equation

T_g = Tax rate applicable to gains and losses on the disposal of fixed assets

T = Corporate income tax rate

n = Number of years covered by the lease agreement

I_j = Interest component of the loan payment

K_s = Salvage value discount rate

O_j = Incremental operating costs of ownership in period t

The interpretation of the *NAL* equation is influenced by the treatment of the key variables in the lease evaluation decision. The seven terms in the *NAL* equation can be interpreted as follows:

1. The purchase price of the asset is an unavoidable cost of purchasing.
2. The present value of the rental payments is a cost of leasing.
3. The present value of the tax shield provided by the rental payments is a benefit of leasing and, consequently, an opportunity cost of purchasing.
4. The present value of the tax shield provided by the depreciation expense is a benefit of purchasing.
5. The present value of the tax shield provided by the interest expense on a "loan equivalent" to a lease is another benefit of purchasing.
6. The present value of the after-tax operating cost is a burden of ownership.
7. The present value of the after-tax residual value is a benefit of ownership.

Summarizing the seven terms, the basic equation provides the net present value advantage of leasing. Setting *NAL* equal to zero and solving for X_i provides the pretax interest rate on the lease. The *NAL* equation can also be explained as follows:

1. The present value of the borrow-and-buy alternative is

$$A_0 - \sum_{j=1}^{n} \frac{TD_j}{(1 + X_3)^j} - \sum_{j=1}^{n} \frac{TI_j}{(1 + X_4)^j} + \sum_{j=1}^{n} \left[\frac{O_j(1 - T)}{(1 + X_5)^j} \right] - \frac{V_n}{(1 + K_s)^j)}$$

2. The present value of leasing is

$$\sum_{j=1}^{n}\frac{R_j}{(1 + X_1)^j} - \sum_{j=1}^{n}\frac{TR_j}{(1 + X_2)^j}.$$

3. NAL = present value of borrowing and buying—present value of leasing. Two problems in the applicability of the NAL equation lie in the choice of the appropriate discount rates to be used and the computation of the loan equivalent to the lease.

The discount rates X_1, X_2, X_3, X_4, and X_5 are those applied by the market to evaluate the streams of distribution of R_j, TR_j, TD_j, TI_j, and $O_j(1-T)$. Possible alternatives are a single discount rate or an appropriate rate for each stream. We will first use the after-tax cost of debt as a single discount rate for all streams; later in the chapter, the other alternatives proposed in the literature will be discussed. Thus, the after-tax cost of debt will be used for each cash flow stream except V_n, which will be discounted at its own rate ($K_s = 20$ percent) due to the uncertainty associated with this "estimated" value.

The loan equivalent decision also has generated a debate in the literature. This chapter will propose a first alternative and later present the other proposed alternatives. For the first alternative, it assumed that

$$P_0 = A_0,$$

$$P_0 = \sum_{j=1}^{n}\frac{L_j}{(1 + r)_j},$$

where

P_0 = Present value of the loan equivalent
L_j = Loan payment at the end of each period j
r = Pretax interest rate on term loans "comparable" to the lease

To illustrate the lessee's analysis, the same problem presented in the lessor's analysis will be used. The data required are as follows:

$A_0 = \$30,000$
$S = \$10,000$
$R_j = \$6,025$ (at the beginning of each period)
$R_j = \$6,507$ (at the end of each period)
D_j = Straight-line depreciation at period $j = \dfrac{A_0 - S}{n} = \$4,000$
$O_j = \$2,000$

$B = 0$

$T_g = 10$ percent

$V_n = S - [(S - B)T_g] = \$9,000$

$r = 6$ percent

$T = 50$ percent

$n = 5$ years

$K_s = 20$ percent

The lessee's analysis proceeds as follows:

1. For the loan payment computation, it has been assumed in this analysis that $P_o = A_o$, and

$$P_o = A_o,$$

$$P_o = \sum_{j=1}^{n} \frac{L_j}{(1 + r)^j},$$

Given a 6 percent interest rate on loans, the amount of the annual loan payment at the end of each year is found by solving the following equation for L_j:

$$\$30,000 = \sum_{j=1}^{5} \frac{L_j}{(1 + 0.06)^j}.$$

$$L_j = \$7,122.$$

2. When the rental payments are made in advance, the lease evaluation analysis proceeds by the computation of the *NAL* as follows:

$$NAL = \$30,000 - \left[\$6,025 + \sum_{j=1}^{4} \frac{\$6,025}{(1 + 0.03)^j}\right] + \sum_{j=1}^{5} \frac{(\$6,025)(0.5)}{(1 + 0.03)^j} - \sum_{j=1}^{5} \frac{(\$4,000)(0.5)}{(1 + 0.03)^j}$$

$$- \left[\frac{\$800(0.5)}{(1 + 0.03)^1} + \frac{\$1,480(0.5)}{(1 + 0.03)^2} + \frac{\$1,142(0.5)}{(1 + 0.03)^3} + \frac{\$783(0.5)}{(1 + 0.03)^4} + \frac{\$403(0.5)}{(1 + 0.03)^5}\right]$$

$$+ \sum_{j=1}^{5} \left[\frac{\$2,000(1 - 0.5)}{(1 + 0.03)^j}\right] - \frac{\$9,000}{(1 + 0.20)^5}$$

$$= \$30,000 - (\$6,025 + \$22,396) + \$13,796 - \$9,159 - \$2,130 + \$4,580 - \$3,617$$

$$= \$5,048 = NAL \text{ when rental payments are made in advance.}$$

3. The lease evaluation analysis when the rental payments are made at the end of the period is as follows:

$$NAL = \$30,000 - \sum_{j=1}^{5}\frac{\$6,057}{(1 + 0.03)^j} + \sum_{j=1}^{5}\frac{(\$6,507(0.5)}{(1 + 0.03)^j} - \sum_{j=1}^{5}\frac{\$4,000(0.5)}{(1 + 0.03)^j}$$

$$- \left[\frac{\$800(0.5)}{(1 + 0.03)^1} + \frac{\$1,480(0.5)}{(1 + 0.03)^2} + \frac{\$1,142(0.5)}{(1 + 0.03)^3} + \frac{\$783(0.5)}{(1 + 0.03)^4} + \frac{\$403(0.05)}{(1 + 0.03)^5}\right]$$

$$+ \sum_{j=1}^{5}\left[\frac{\$2,000(1 - 0.5)}{(1 + 0.03)^j}\right] - \frac{\$9,000}{(1 + 0.20)^5}$$

$$= \$30,000 - \$29,800 + \$14,900 - \$9,159 - \$2,130 + \$4,580 - \$3,167$$

$$= \$4,774 = NAL \text{ when rental payments are made at the end of the period.}$$

These computations show the lease alternative to be preferable to the purchase alternative. Several points should be further emphasized:

1. Changing the depreciation method from straight-line to accelerated depreciation may change the outcome.
2. The timing of the rental payments has an impact on the *NAL*.
3. The analysis assumes that the acquisition price of the asset is equal to the principal of the loan.
4. All the cash flow streams except for the salvage value are discounted at the after-tax cost of debt.
5. It is assumed that the investment decision has been deemed acceptable. Only the financing decision remains to be evaluated in terms of a choice between borrowing and leasing.

ALTERNATIVE CALCULATIONS

The Johnson and Lewellen Approach

R. W. Johnson and W. G. Lewellen examined (1) whether the financing and investment decisions should be mixed in appraising lease possibilities and (2) which discount rate should be used.[6] (See Exhibit 1.1 for all of the approaches to lease evaluation.)

Johnson and Lewellen pose the decision problem as a lease-or-buy rather than a lease-or-borrow decision, since a lease contract is simply an arrangement for the long-term acquisition of service, which does not differ in financing terms from the alternative acquisition-of-service arrangement called purchase. Hence the inclusion of a charge for interest as a "cost" of owning is viewed as a deficiency of current models for lease evaluation, and the concept of a loan equivalent is not necessary in the lease evaluation model.

The issue of the appropriate rate to use in discounting the cash flows relevant to the decision has been investigated by Johnson and Lewellen. They emphasize the following ideas:

1. The after-tax cash flows with predictability matching that associated with a firm's debt service obligations should be capitalized at the firm's after-tax borrowing rate (after-tax cost of debt). This will include the obligations incurred under the lease contract, such as lease payments and their respective tax savings.

2. The after-tax cash flows with uncertainty like the general risks faced by the firm in its line of business should be discounted at the firm's cost of capital. This will include the depreciation tax shield, the after-tax operating costs, and the salvage value.

The Johnson and Lewellen model now can be presented. It states

$$\Delta NPV = NPV(P) - NPV(L) = \sum_{j=1}^{n} \left[\frac{D_j T - O_j(1 - T)}{(1 + K)^j} \right]$$
$$+ \frac{V_n}{(1 + K)^j} - A_0 + \sum_{j=1}^{n} \frac{R_j(1 - T)}{[1 + r(1 - T)]}$$

where

ΔNPV = Change in the firm's net present value

$NPV(P)$ = The net present value of borrowing and buying

$NPV(L)$ = The net present value of leasing

K = Cost of capital at 12 percent

A positive value of *NPV* would imply that purchasing the asset is economically superior to leasing it. This would occur if the net salvage value exceeded after-tax operating costs or if the purchase price less depreciation tax savings were less than the burden of lease payments. Using the data in the previous illustration, the Johnson and Lewellen model proceeds as follows:

1. If the rental payments are made at the beginning of the period,

Exhibit 1.1
Approaches to Lease Evaluation

Approach	Summary measure	Excluded flows or other comments	Equivalent loan calculation*	Discount rate used for:					
				X_2	X_3	X_4	X_5	X_6	X_7
Beechy [1,3]	1	tL_j is used instead of tR_j in the 3rd term of the equation.	$P_O = A_O$ $B_O = \sum_{j=0}^{n} (R_j/(1+r)j)$ $L_j = R_j(P_O/B_O)$	1	1	1	1	1	1
Bower, Herringer, Williamson [4]	NAL		$P_O = \dot{A}_O$ $B_O = \sum_{j=0}^{n} (R_j/(1+r)j)$ $L_j = R_j(P_O/B_O)$	r	k	k	k	k	k
Doenges [5] Mitchell [8] Wyman [12]	$i(1-t)$	I_j is excluded. Wyman provides a probability distribution of rates.	None	$i(1-t)$	$i(1-t)$	$i(1-t)$	–	$i(1-t)$	$i(1-t)$
Findlay [6]	NAL	Certainty equivalents of O_j and V_n are used in the 6th and 7th terms.	$P_O = \sum_{j=0}^{n} (R_j/(1+r)j)$ $L_j = R_j$	r	$r(1-t)$	$r(1-t)$	$r(1-t)$	$r(1-t)$	$r(1-t)$

Approach									
Johnson and Lewellen [7]	NAL	I_j is excluded.	None	$r(1-t)$	$r(1-t)$	k	—	k	k
Roenfeldt and Osteryoung [10]	$i(1-t)$	I_j is excluded. Certainty equivalents of O_j and V_n are used in the 6th and 7th terms.	None	$i(1-t)$	$i(1-t)$	$i(1-t)$	$i(1-t)$	k	$i(1-t)$
Vancil [11]	NAL	$P_o = A_o$ $L_j = R_j$	r	k	k	k	k		

*Only the first two or three equations required to produce the equivalent loan flows are shown in each box. The remaining equations are the same for each approach. The full set of equations for Beechey's approach is:

$$P_o = A_o$$
$$B_o = \sum_{j=o}^{n} (R_j/(1+r)^j)$$

$$L_j = R_j (P_o/B_o)$$
$$I_j = rP_{j-1}$$

$$Q_j = L_j - I_j$$
$$P_j = P_{j-1} - Q_j.$$

Source: R. S. Bower, "Issues in Lease Financing," *Financial Management* (Winter 1973), p. 27. Reprinted with permission, Financial Management Association, College of Business Administration #3331, University of South Florida, Tampa, FL 33620–5500, 813–974–2084.

$$\Delta NPV = \sum_{j=1}^{5}\left[\frac{\$2,000-\$1,000}{(1+0.12)^j}\right] + \frac{\$9,000}{(1+0.12)^{-5}} - \$30,000 + \left[\$6,025 + \sum_{j=1}^{4}\frac{\$6,025}{1.03^j}\right]$$

$$- \sum_{j=1}^{5}\left[\frac{\$6,025(1-0.5)}{(1+0.03)^j}\right] = \$(6,664).$$

Thus, leasing is preferred.

2. If the rental payments are made at the end of the period,

$$\Delta NPV = \sum_{j=1}^{5}\left[\frac{\$2,000-\$1,000}{(1+0.12)^j}\right] + \frac{\$9,000}{(1+0.12)^5} - \$30,000 + \sum_{j=1}^{5}\left[\frac{\$6,507}{1.03^j}\right]$$

$$- \sum_{j=1}^{5}\left[\frac{\$6,507(1-0.5)}{(1+0.03)^j}\right] = \$(6,388).$$

Leasing is preferred in this case as well.

As a result of discounting the costs of financing at $r(1-T)$ and the ownership cash flows at K, the Johnson and Lewellen approach in this case creates a bias in favor of leasing. R. S. Bower contested the choice:

Johnson and Lewellen's selection of K as the discount rate is understandable but unappealing. It is understandable because K is the rate used in discounting depreciation shelters in conventional capital budgeting, where the shelter is part of the cash flow calculation. The selection of K is unappealing, though, because it involves discounting some of the tax shelter given up in leasing at a high rate, K, and discounting all of the tax shelter that comes with leasing at a low rate, $r(1-T)$. It is difficult to avoid the conclusion that a higher discount rate for the shelter element of lease cost does a great deal more to bias the analysis in favor of leasing than it does to recognize any real difference in risk.[7]

The Roenfeldt and Osteryoung Approach

The Roenfeldt and Osteryoung approach expanded on the Johnson and Lewellen approach by categorically separating the investment decision from the financing decision.[8] The methodology used consisted of (1) determining the desirability of the investment decision, and (2) given that the investment decision was deemed desirable, evaluating the financing decision by comparing the after-tax cost of borrowing (r_b) with the after-tax cost of leasing (r_l). Using the data from the illustration in the previous section, the Ronefeldt and Osteryoung approach proceeds as follows.

Step 1: The Investment Decision

The investment decision is made on the basis of a net present value or internal rate of return approach following traditional capital budgeting techniques (see chapter 5). The computation of a net present value or internal rate of return involves estimating the annual sales generated by the asset and computing the resulting net cash flows, as follows:

		Year				
	0	*1*	*2*	*3*	*4*	*5*
1. Sales (Assumed)		$20,000	$20,000	$20,000	$20,000	$20,000
2. Depreciation		4,000	4,000	4,000	4,000	4,000
3. Cash Operating Costs		2,000	2,000	2,000	2,000	2,000
4. Taxable Income (Line 1 − Line 2 − Line 3)		14,000	14,000	14,000	14,000	14,000
5. Tax Liability ($4 \times T$)		7,000	7,000	7,000	7,000	7,000
6. Net Cash Flow (Line 1 − Line 5 − Line 3)		11,000	11,000	11,000	11,000	11,000
7. Salvage Value (V_n)						9,000
8. Discount Factor ($K = 12$)						3.605
9. Discount Factor ($K_s = 20$)						0.402
10. Present Value of Cash Flow						39,655
11. Present Value of V_n						3,618
12. Total Present Value (Line 10 + Line 11)						$43,273

Thus, the net present value is equal to $13,273, or $43,273 − $30,000, and the investment is deemed desirable.

Step 2: The Financing Decision

The financing decision—to borrow or to lease—is made on the basis of a criterion of least cost by comparing the after-tax cost of borrowing (r_b) to the after-tax cost of leasing (r_l). To compute r_b, the rate that equates the after-tax interest payments and amortization of the principal to the loan amount, the following formula is used:

$$A_0 = \sum_{j=1}^{n} \frac{L_j - I_j T}{(1 + r_b)^j},$$

or

$$\$30,000 = \sum_{j=1}^{5} \frac{\$7,122 - [0.5(I_j)]}{(1 + r_b)^j}.$$

The numerator (the net costs of borrowing) is computed as follows:

Year	Loan Payment	Interest	Interest Tax Shield ($I_j T$)	Net Cost of Borrowing
1	$7,122	$1,800	$900.00	$6,222.00
2	7,122	1,480	740.00	6,382.00
3	7,122	1,142	571.00	6,551.00
4	7,122	783	391.50	6,730.50
5	7,122	403	201.50	6,920.50

Solving for r_b yields $r_b = 3$ percent. To compute r_i, the rate that equates the adjusted rental payments to the cost of the asset (A_0), Roenfeldt and Osteryoung make the following changes:

1. The rental payments are reduced by the amount of any operating costs assumed by the lessor.
2. The depreciation tax shield and after-tax salvage value are added to the cost of leasing.
3. Certainty equivalents are introduced into the operating and residual cash flows to adjust for risk.

The following formula is then used:

$$V_0 = \left(\sum_{j=1}^{n} \frac{[(L_j - \grave{a}_j O_j)(1 - T)] + D_j T}{(1 + r_1)^n} \right) + \left[\frac{{}^{\grave{a}}_n S_n - (\grave{a}_n S_n - B) T_g}{(1 + r_1)^n} \right]$$

where

$\grave{a}_j$ = Certainty equivalent for the operating costs
$\grave{a}_n$ = Certainty equivalent for the salvage value

Assuming $\grave{a}_j = 0.6$ and $\grave{a}_n = 0.99$, the cost of leasing (r_l) can be computed as follows:

1. If the rental payments are made at the end of the period,

$$\$30,000 = \left\{ \sum_{j=1}^{5} \frac{[\$6,507 - 0.6(\$2,000)](1 - 0.5) + [(\$4,000)(0.5)]}{(1 + r_l)^n} \right\}$$

$$+ \left\{ \frac{0.99(\$10,000) - [0.99(\$10,000) - 0](0.10)}{(1 + r_l)^n} \right\}$$

$$= \sum_{j=1}^{5} \left[\frac{\$4,653.5}{(1 + r_l)^n} \right] + \left[\frac{\$8,910}{(1 + r_l)^5} \right]$$

$r_l = 2$ percent, and leasing is preferable to borrowing.

2. If the rental payments are in advance,

$$\$30,000 = \left\{ \sum_{j=0}^{4} \frac{[\$6,025 - 0.6(\$2,000)](1 - 0.5) + [(\$4,000)(0.5)]}{(1 + r_l)^n} \right\} + \left[\frac{\$8,910}{(1 + r_l)^5} \right]$$

$r_l = 2.1$ percent, and leasing is still preferable to borrowing.

Issues in Lease Financing

Bower summarized the following points of agreement and disagreement in the differing approaches to the lease-or-buy decision.[9] All the models require inputs that include the purchase price of the asset to be leased (A_o), lease payments at the end or at the beginning of the period (R_j), a depreciation charge relevant for tax payments at the end of the period (D_j), a cash operating cost expected to occur in period I if the asset is purchased but not if it is leased (O_j), an expected after-tax salvage value of the asset at the end of the last period covered by the lease agreement (V_n), a pretax interest rate on the loan equivalent to the lease (r), an after-tax cost of capital for the corporation (k), a corporate income tax rate (T), and the number of periods covered by the lease agreement (n).

The points of disagreement relating to the lease-or-buy analysis include the following:

1. The choice of a summary measure, either the pretax interest rate on a lease (I) or the net advantage to a lease (NAL).

2. The inclusion or exclusion of some of the terms previously presented in the normative model.

3. The computation of the loan equivalent.

4. The choice of a discount rate for each of the cash flows included in the normative model.

The Bower Approach: A Decision Format

Bower has developed a decision format to reconcile the disagreements among the various approaches to the lease-or-buy analysis and still permit those interested to take advantage of the model's broad agreement on other points. The decision format examines the decision implications associated with different tax shelter discount rates.

The decision format uses the cost of capital (K) to calculate benefits that involve the purchase price, operating savings, and salvage value; it uses the appropriate interest rate (r) to calculate the present cost of the lease payments. The tax shelter effect is then calculated for rate of discount (X) from 0 through 14 percent.

The cost of purchasing (COP) depends on the purchase price, depreciation tax shelter, cash operating cost avoided by leasing, and salvage value:

$$COP = A_0 - \sum_{j=0}^{n}\left[\frac{TD_j}{(1 + X)^j}\right] + \sum_{j=0}^{n}\left[\frac{O_j(1 - T)}{(1 + K)^j}\right] - \frac{V_n}{(1 + K)^n}.$$

The cost of leasing (COL) depends on the lease payment, lease tax shelter, and the interest tax shelter lost by leasing:

$$COL = \sum_{j=0}^{n}\left[\frac{R_j}{(1 + r)^j}\right] - \sum_{j=0}^{n}\left[\frac{TR_j}{(1 + X)^j}\right] + \sum_{j=0}^{n}\left[\frac{TI_j}{(1 + X)^j}\right].$$

An illustrative example of Bower's decision format will be given using the data presented in the example in the "Lessor's Analysis" section. There is, however, one major change: The lease payments (R_j), as calculated in the lessor's analysis, will no longer be used. The equivalent loan is computed by Bower as follows:

$$\text{Loan equivalent } (P_0) = \sum_{j=1}^{n} \frac{R_j}{(1 + r)^j},$$

where

R_j (Lease payment) = Loan payment (L_j).

r = Pretax interest rate on term loans "comparable" to the lease.

Although most of the data supplied in the original example applies here, assume that as an alternative to purchasing, the asset can be leased for five years for a payment of $7,962 per annum. In this case, the lease equivalent no longer equals the purchase price of the asset; instead, the following holds true:

$$\text{Loan equivalent } (P_0) = \sum_{j=1}^{n} \frac{\$7,962}{(1 + 0.06)^j} = \$33,538.$$

The loan equivalent is:

Year	Loan Payment	Loan Balance (Year Start)	Interest	Principal Repayment	Loan Balance (Year-End)
1	$7,962	$33,538	$2,012	$5,950	$27,588
2	7,962	27,588	1,655	6,307	21,281
3	7,962	21,281	1,277	6,685	14,596
4	7,962	14,596	876	7,086	7,510
5	7,962	7,510	452	7,511	0

The decision format is presented in Exhibits 1.2 and 1.3. The columns at the right in Exhibit 1.2 show that when the tax shelter is discounted at $r(1-T)=10$ percent, the net advantage of purchasing is $49. At all discount rates above 9.65 percent, the lease has a net disadvantage. Therefore, if a decision maker analyzing a graph such as Exhibit 1.3 believes that the proper tax shelter discount rate lies well below the intersection point, the decision to lease rather than purchase would provide the greater financial benefit to the company.

In developing this decision format, Bower has devised a composite approach to the lease-or-buy decision that enables the executive to make a judgment on the principal disagreement among academicians and on

Exhibit 1.2
Decision Format Table

| Year t | Purchase Price A_t | Lease Payment $R_t = L_t$ | Tax Shelter | | | After-Tax Operating Saving $O_t(1-t)$ | After-Tax Salvage V_s |
			Lease Payment TR_t	Depreciation TD_t	Loan Interest TI_t		
0	30,000						
1		7,962	3,981	2,000	1,006	1,000	
2		7,962	3,981	2,000	828	1,000	
3		7,962	3,981	2,000	638	1,000	
4		7,962	3,981	2,000	438	1,000	
5		7,962	3,981	2,000	226	1,000	9,000

Present Value at
| $k = 0.12$ | 30,000 | | | | | 3,605 | 5,107 |
| $r = 0.06$ | | 33,538 | | | | | |

| | | | | | Cost of | |
					Purchasing	Leasing
0	19,905	10,000	3,136		18,498	16,769
0.02	18,764	9,427	2,993		19,071	17,767
0.04	17,223	8,904	2,868		19,594	19,183
0.06	17,769	8,425	2,737		20,073	19,506
0.08	15,895	7,985	2,624		20,513	20,267
0.10	15,091	7,582	2,518		20,916	20,965
0.12	14,351	7,210	2,419		21,288	21,606
0.14	13,667	6,866	2,327		21,632	22,198

how the proper tax shelter discount rate, $r(1-T)$, may affect the ultimate cost of a decision.

CONCLUSION

A firm may enter into a leasing arrangement for many reasons. Some of the primary motivations follow:

1. Leasing enables a firm to take advantage of tax shelters.
2. A leasing arrangement conserves working capital.
3. Cash budgeting benefits, because leasing permits accurate predictions of cash needs.
4. Leasing allows a company to retain a degree of flexibility lost by debt financing (that is, bond indenture sometimes imposes restrictions on future financing).
5. A leasing arrangement provides convenience.

Exhibit 1.3
Decision Format Graph

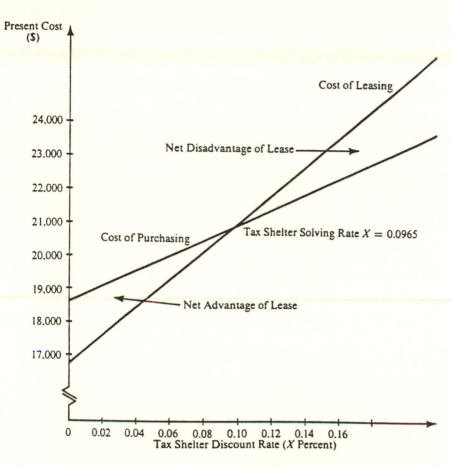

6. Leasing can provide an economical means of obtaining excellent servicing and maintenance of equipment if a maintenance lease is included.

7. An operating lease provides more flexibility than ownership if the asset becomes unprofitable; it avoids part or all of the risk of obsolescence; and it can provide for modern equipment from year to year.

Most of the significant methods of analyzing lease-or-buy alternatives use the same basic formula for calculation, but there is considerable disagreement in the calculation methods. The disagreement lies with both relevant alternatives and the choice of the best summary measure of comparison. The relevant alternatives include the outstanding principal of the loan equivalent, the principal component, the present value of the lease claim, and the discount rates to be applied to cash flows in each category, which are intended to reflect opportunity cost. Summary measures are either the increment in net present value of owners, wealth, or the after-tax interest rate on the lease.

The disagreement is more significant in the treatment of the terms, including lease payments and the tax shelter acquired or given up if the lease is accepted. This is most obvious in the decision to include or exclude the tax deduction associated with interest on the equivalent loan.

Bower's decision form of lease analysis is the most appropriate method to use today. It is a composite of the factors agreed upon by other theorists, and it enables decision makers to choose the cost of capital and interest rate they feel is most appropriate during the relevant period for making their lease-or-buy decisions. Bower's decision format also enables decision makers to see the effects of their costs and rates and make their decisions in light of the uncertainty of these factors.

APPENDIX

QUESTIONS

1. Analysis of the Lease-or-Buy Decision: The Johnson and Lewellen Approach

The Holland Consulting Company is considering obtaining a piece of equipment having a five-year useful life and costing $15,000. As an alternative to purchasing, the company can lease the equipment for five years for a payment of $4,200 per annum. The equipment, which would be fully depreciated on a sum-of-the-years'-digits schedule, is expected to command a $1,500 cash salvage value at the end of year 5 and will require $1,000 more in annual (pretax) operating costs if it is owned rather than leased. The Holland Consulting Company is also assuming the corporate income tax rate to be 50 percent, the capital gains tax rate to be 30 percent, the cost of capital after taxes to be 12 percent, and the pretax effective interest rate to be 8 percent.

Required: Should Holland Consulting Company lease or buy the equipment? (Use the Johnson and Lewellen approach.)

2. Analysis of the Lease-or-Buy Decision: A Decision Format

Assume the same data as in question 1. This time, the Holland Consulting Company has decided to modify the Johnson and Lewellen approach as follows:

1. It will apply the cost of capital to the purchase price, after-tax operating savings, and after-tax salvage value.
2. It will apply the after-tax rate of interest to the lease payment, the lease payment tax shelter, and the depreciation tax shelter.
3. It will apply an after-tax rate of interest from 0 to 14 percent.

Required: Should the Holland Company lease or buy equipment?

3. Analysis of the Lease-or-Buy Decision: Another Decision Format

Assume the same data as in question 1. This time, the Holland Consulting Company has decided to modify the Johnson and Lewellen approach as follows:

1. A loan equivalent is introduced in the evaluation. Findlay's loan equivalent formula is to be used.
2. The cost of purchasing depends on the purchase price, depreciation tax shelter, cash operating cost avoided by leasing, and salvage value.
3. The cost of leasing depends on the lease payment, lease tax shelter, and interest tax shelter lost by leasing.
4. The after-tax salvage and the after-tax operating savings are discounted at the cost of capital.
5. The lease payments are discounted at the pretax rate of interest.
6. The tax shelters are discounted at a rate of interest 0 to 14 percent.

Required:

1. Determine the loan equivalent schedule using Findlay's equivalent loan.
2. Compute the costs of purchasing and costs of leasing, and determine if the Holland Consulting Company should lease or buy the equipment.

4. Comparison of Lease Evaluation Models

The Richard Company is contemplating the addition of a truck to its commercial truck fleet. The truck costs $56,000, which does not include transportation costs of $4,000. The Richard Company has a policy of capitalizing freight in the determination of the acquisition cost. The truck has an estimated three-year useful life and a $2,000 residual value. Other relevant information for deciding whether to lease or buy the truck includes the following:

Borrowing rate: 6 percent

Cost of capital before taxes: 20 percent

Tax rate: 50 percent

Depreciation method: sum-of-the-years'-digits method

Rate of return on investment desired: 10 percent

Salvage value discount rate: 20 percent

Required:

1. From the lessor's perspective, determine the annual rental payment if paid in advance.
2. From the lessor's perspective, determine the annual rental payment if paid at the end of the period.
3. Present the normative model to be used by the lessee. What is required to express the model as an advantage to ownership?
4. Determine the loan payment on a loan equivalent to the lease.
5. From the lessee's perspective, should the Richard Company lease the equipment if the rental payment is made at the beginning of the period?

6. From the lessee's perspective, should the Richard Company lease the equipment if the rental payment is made at the end of the period?

7. Present the Johnson and Lewellen model that can be used by the lessee.

8. Repeat part 6 using the Johnson and Lewellen model.

ANSWERS

1. Analysis of the Lease-or-Buy Decision: The Johnson and Lewellen Approach

To decide whether to lease or buy, the Holland Consulting Company should proceed as follows:

	(1)	(2)	(3)	(4)	(5)	(6)
	Tax Savings on Depreciation	After Tax Added Operating Costs	Salvage Value, Net of Taxes,	After Tax Lease Payment	Present Value of $(1)-(2)+(3)$	Present Value of
Year	$(t\ D_j)$	$Q\ (1-T)$	V_n	$L_i\ (1-t)$	at 12%	(4) at 4%
1	(.5) 5,000	(.5) 1,000		(.5) (4,200)	$1,786	$2,019
2	(.5) 4,000	(.5) 1,000		(.5) (4,200)	1,196	1,942
3	(.5) 3,000	(.5) 1,000		(.5) (4,200)	712	1,867
4	(.5) 2,000	(.5) 1,000		(.5) (4,200)	318	1,795
5	(.5) 1,000	(.5) 1,000	(.70) (1,500)	(.5) (4,200)	596	1,726
					$4,608	$9,349

Equipment Purchase = $15,000
Therefore $\Delta\ NPV$ = $4,608 − $15,000 + $9,439 = −$1,043
Conclusion = leasing is better than purchase.

2. Analysis of the Lease-or-Buy Decision: A Decision Format

To decide whether to lease or buy, the Holland Consulting Company should proceed as follows:

Evaluation: The purchase price net of salvage and the operating expenses that will now be covered by the lessor are the benefits associated with leasing. The lease payments, less any net additional tax shelter they

provide, are the costs of leasing. The benefits which are discounted at
the cost of capital, are $16,206. The benefits in question appear and are
graphed in the following table:

			Tax Shelter			
Year j	Purchase Price A_o	Lease Payment R_i	Lease Payment tR_i	Depreciation tD_i	After-Tax Operating Saving $O_i(1-t)$	After Salvage V_n
0	$15,000					
1		$4,200	$2,100	$2,500	$500	
2		4,200	2,100	2,000	500	
3		4,200	2,100	1,500	500	
4		4,200	2,100	1,000	500	
5		4,200	2,100	500	500	$1,050
PV $K=.12$	$15,000				$1,802	−$596

				Lease	
				Benefit	Cost
				$16,206 (@12%)	
.0	−$21,000	+$10,500	−$7,500		$18,000
.02	−19,797	+ 9,898	−7,164		17,063
.04	−18,698	+ 9,349	−6,852		16,201
.06	−17,692	+ 8,846	−6,564		15,410
.08	−16,769	+ 8,385	−6,296		14,680
.10	−15,921	+ 7,961	−6,046		14,006
.12	−15,140	+ 7,570	−5,813		13,383
.14	−14,119	+ 7,209	−5,596		12,806

$t = .5, k = .12, r = .08$

This table also shows the costs of the lease discounted at various rates;
therefore, they satisfy preference for both present value and internal rate
of return summary measures.

This lease has a net disadvantage at after-tax interest rates below .0399
and a net advantage at rates above this figure. At .04, the after-tax interest

rate provided in the case, the net advantage is $5. The decision format indicates a borderline choice in favor of the lease or, more pragmatically, a choice that should make very little difference to the owners of the lessee corporation even if the executives are using 8 percent as the appropriate pre-tax borrowing rate when that rate is correctly 6 percent or 10 percent.

In conclusion, this format offers to the executive table and a graph (Exhibits 1.2 and 1.3) which took the cost of capital as given in calculating the benefits of leasing and assumed that tax shelters should be discounted at the after-tax rate of interest and allows the executive to examine the decision implication associated with different interest rates.

3. Analysis of the Lease or Buy Decision: Another Decision Format

A. The loan is calculated as Findlay's loan equivalent. The loan schedule is:

Year	Loan Balance, Beginning of Year	Interest at 8%	Principal	Loan Balance, Year End
1	$16,769	$1,342	$2,858	$13,911
2	13,911	1,113	3,087	10,823
3	10,823	866	3,334	7,489
4	7,489	599	3,601	3,888
5	3,888	311	3,889	

B. The decision format applied to this problem appears as follows:

				Tax Shelter			
Year j	Purchase Price A_o	Lease Payment R_i	Lease Payment tR_i	Depreciation tD_i	Loan Interest* tI_i	After-Tax Operating Saving $O_i(1-t)$	After-Tax Salvage V_n
0	$15,000						
1		$4,200	$2,100	$2,500	$671	$500	

Tax Shelter (*continued*)

Year j	Purchase Price A_o	Lease Payment R_i	Lease Payment tR_i	Depreciation tD_i	Loan Interest* tI_i	After-Tax Operating Saving $O_i(1-t)$	After-Tax Salvage V_n
2		4,200	2,100	2,000	556	500	
3		4,200	2,100	1,500	433	500	
4		4,200	2,100	1,000	300	500	
5		4,200	2,100	500	156	500	$1,050

$t = .5, k = .12, r = .08$

						Cost of	
$\dfrac{PV*}{}$							
K=.12 $15,000						Purchasing	Leasing
r=.08	$16,769						
0		$10,500	$7,500	$2,116	$ 8,706	$ 8,385	
.02		9,898	7,164	2,019	9,042	8,890	
.04		9,349	6,852	1,929	9,354	9,349	
.06		8,846	6,564	1,846	9,642	9,769	
.08		8,385	6,296	1,768	9,910	10,152	
.10		7,961	6,046	1,697	10,160	10,505	
.12		7,570	5,813	1,630	10,393	10,829	
.14		7,209	5,596	1,567	10,610	11,127	

*The loan is calculated as Findlay's equivalent loan. The loan schedule is:

Year	Loan Balance, Beginning of Year	Interest at 8%	Principal	Loan Balance, Year End
1	$16,769	$1,342	$2,858	$13,911
2	13,911	1,113	3,087	10,823
3	10,823	866	3,334	7,489
4	7,489	599	3,601	3,888
5	3,888	311	3,889	

*PV of After-Tax Operating Savings = $1,802
*PV of After-Tax Salvage Value   = $ 596

4. Normative Model for Lease Evaluation

A. The lessor determines first the present value of the residual as follows:

$$S_{PV} = \frac{S}{(1+R)^{-t}}$$

$$= \frac{2,000}{(1+.20)^{-3}} = \$1,158$$

Then, the rental (X), if paid in advance

$$C - S = X_1 + \sum_{t=2}^{3} \frac{X_t}{(1+R)^{t-1}}$$

$$= \$60,000 - 1,158 = X_1 + \frac{X_2}{(1+.10)} + \frac{X_3}{(1+.10)^2}$$

$$X = \$21,056$$

B. The rental (X), if paid at end of period, may be computed as follows:

$$C - S = \sum_{t=1}^{n} \frac{X_t}{(1+R)^t} \text{ or } \$60,000 - \$1,158 = \sum_{t=1}^{n} \frac{X_t}{(1+.10)^t}$$

$$X = \$23,660$$

C. The normative model to be used by the lessee is as follows:

$$NAL = \sum_{t=1}^{n} \frac{P - (I_t + D_t)\, T_c}{(1+K_d)^t} + \frac{O_t(1-T_c)}{(1+K_d)^t} - S - \frac{(S-B)T_g}{(1+K_s)}$$

$$- \sum_{t=1}^{n} \frac{L_t(1-T_c)}{(1+K_d)^t}$$

Where:

P = the loan payment: interest and amortization of principal
L_t = the rental payment in period t
I_t = interest payment in period t
D_t = depreciation in period t

O_t = incremental operating costs of ownership in period t

T_c = ordinary corporate tax rate

T_g = tax rate applicable to gains and losses on the disposal of fixed assets

S_n = expected cash value of asset in period N

B = book value of asset in period N

K_d = explicit after-tax cost of new debt capital

K = weighted average cost of capital, after tax

K_s = discount rate applied to residual values

D. The loan payment is found by:

$$\$60,000 = \sum_{t=1}^{n} \frac{L_t}{(1 + .06)^t}$$

$$L_t = \$22,447$$

The loan schedule is as follows:

Year	Payment (L_t)	Interest (I_t)	Principal	Balance
1	$22,447	$3,600	$18,847	$41,153
2	22,447	2,469	19,978	21,175
3	22,447	1,270	21,175	—

E. Lessee's analysis when rental payments are made in advance:

Year	0	1	2	3	Explanations
1. Loan Payment		$22,447	$22,447	$22,447	
2. Interest		3,600	2,469	1,270	
3. Depreciation		29,000	19,140	9,860	
4. Tax Deduction (2+3)		32,600	21,609	11,130	
5. Tax Shield (4×.50)		16,300	10,804	5,565	
6. Net Ownership (1−5)		6,147	11,643	16,882	
7. After Tax Lease Cost	$10,753	10,753	10,753		

Year	0	1	2	3	Explanations
8. Advantage to Ownership	10,753	4,606	(910)	{(16,882)2,000}	Salvage Value
9. Discount Factor $(K_d = 3\%)$		.971	.943	{.915,.579}	$K_s = 20\%$
10. Present Value of Owner	10,753	4,472	(858)	{(15,4771,158}	
11. Advantage to Ownership				78	

F. Lessee's analysis when rental payments are made at end of period:

Year	0	1	2	3	Explanations
Row 1 to 6 are similar to the previous lessee's analysis					
7. After Tax Lease Cost	—	$11,830	$11,830	$11,830	
8. Advantage to Ownership	—	5,683	187	(5,052)	
8a. S				2,000	(Salvage Value)
9. Discount Factor $(K_d=3\%)$		.971	.941	.915	
9a. $(K_s=20\%)$				.579	
10. Present Value of Owning		$5,518	179	(4,623)	
10.a S				1,158	
11. Advantage to Ownership				2,229	

G. Johnson and Lewellen's model states:

$$\Delta NPV = NPV\,(P) - NPV\,(L) = \sum_{t=1}^{n} \frac{D_t T - O_t(1-T)}{(1+K)^t} + \frac{S - T_g\,(S-B)}{(1+K)^n}$$
$$- A_o + \sum_{t=1}^{n} \frac{L_t\,(1-T)}{(1+K_d)^t}$$

Where

$$\Delta NPV = \text{change in the firm's } NPV$$
$$NPV\ (P) = \text{the } NPV \text{ of borrow and buy}$$
$$NPV\ (L) = \text{the } NPV \text{ of leasing}$$

H. The lessee's analysis using Johnson and Lewellen's model proceeds as follows:

Year	0	1	2	3	Total
1. Depreciation Tax Shield	—	$14,500	$ 9,570	$ 4,930	
2. Salvage				2,000	
3. After-Tax Lease Cost		11,830	11,830	11,830	
4. Discount Factor ($K=10\%$)		.909	.826	.751	
5. Present Value of Ownership		13,180	7,904	3,702 1,502	$26,288 (Salvage)
6. Discount Factor ($K_d=3\%$)		.971	.943	.915	
7. Present Value of Leasing		11,487	11,156	10,824	33,467

Therefore, ΔNPV = $26,288 − $60,000 + $33,467 = ($245). Leasing is preferred.

NOTES

1. For a discussion of leverage leasing, see Robert C. War, "Economic Implications of Multiple Rates of Return in the Leverage Lease Context," *Journal of Finance* (December 1973), pp. 275–286; and E. Richard Packham, "An Analysis of the Risks of Leverage Leasing," *Journal of Commercial Bank Lending* (March 1975), pp. 2–29.

2. D. R. Grant, "Illusion in Lease Financing," *Harvard Business Review* (March-April 1959), p. 129.

3. Ibid., p. 126.

4. R. V. Vamco, "Lease or Borrow: New Method of Analysis," *Harvard Business Review* (September-October 1961), p. 127.

5. Financial Accounting Standards Board, *Accounting for the Sale or Purchase of Tax Benefits through Tax Leases, Exposure Draft* (Stamford, Conn: FASB, November 30, 1981), p. 11.

6. R. W. Johnson and W. G. Lewellen, "Analysis of the Lease or Buy Decision," *Journal of Finance* (September 1972), pp. 815–823.

7. R. S. Bower, "Issues in Lease Financing," *Financial Management* (Winter 1973), p. 129.

8. R. L. Roenfeldt and J. S. Osteryoung, "Analysis of Financial Leases," *Financial Management* (Spring 1973), pp. 74–87.

9. Bower, "Issue in Lease Financing," p. 27.

SELECTED READINGS

Beechy, T. H. "The Cost of Leasing: Comment and Correction." *Accounting Review* (October 1970), pp. 769–773.

Beechy, T. H. "Quasi-Debt Analysis of Financial Leases." *Accounting Review* (April 1969), pp. 375–381.

Billiam, Phillip L. "Lease versus Purchase: A Practical Problem." *Cost and Management* (September-October 1974), pp. 32–36.

Bower, R. S., F. C. Herringer, and J. P. Williamson. "Lease Evaluation." *Accounting Review* (April 1966), pp. 257–265.

Burns, Jane O. and Kathleen Bindon. "Evaluating Leases with LP." *Management Accounting* (February 1980), pp. 48–53.

2

Accounting for Long-Term Leases: Part I

INTRODUCTION

Leasing is quickly becoming one of the most popular ways of financing fixed asset acquisitions, producing funds for about a third of the externally purchased capital equipment in the United States. As defined in the Financial Accounting Standards Board's (FASB) *Statement No. 13 as Amended and Interpreted through January 1990,* a lease is an agreement convening the right to use property, plant, or equipment (land or depreciable assets or both) usually for a stated period of time.[1] The lessor is the owner giving up the right to use the property, plant, and equipment and the lessee is the one acquiring the right.

Up to the 1960s, firms had the option of reporting the lease information in the notes or disclosing nothing. Other options included either capitalizing the lease if it conveys some ownership rights and privileges, or expensing the lease payment if it does not convey these rights and privileges. The capitalizing proposals included various views such as capitalize those leases similar to installment purchases, capitalize all long-term leases,[2] and capitalize firm leases when the penalty for nonperformance is substantial.[3] The FASB voted for the capitalization approach when the lease transfers substantially all the risks and benefits of the ownership, representing in substance a purchase by the lessee and a sale by the lessor. The capitalization applies to noncancellable leases. The capitalization of the present value of future rental payments dictates that the lessee recognizes an asset (leased equipment) and a liability (lease obligation), and the lessor recognizes a receivable (net lease receivable) and a credit to equipment. More entries that are required depending on the complexity of the situation are treated in the remainder of this chapter.

ADVANTAGES OF LEASING

The popularity and growth of leasing is best explained by its advantages. They include:

1. *Financing advantage* in the form of 100 percent financing at fixed rates and without a down payment and more flexible than debt agreements.

2. *Reduction of the risk of obsolescence* to the lessee that may include in some cases the transfer of the risk in residual value to the lessor.

3. *Tax advantages* through the deduction of the lease payments or a write-off of the full cost of the asset.

4. *Alternative minimum tax problems* may turn the alternative minimum tax (AMT) to our advantage. As explained by Donald Kieso and Jerry Weygandt: "under the AMT rules, a portion of accelerated depreciation deductions are considered tax preference items that are added to a company's regular taxable income to arrive at the alternative minimum taxable income (AMTI). The company must pay whichever is higher, the regular tax or the AMT. Since ownership of equipment can't contribute to an increased AMTI and, ultimately, to an alternative minimum tax liability in access of the regular tax liabilities, companies often find leasing a way to avoid the owners alternative tax provisions."[4]

5. *Balance sheet advantages* are realized through the absorption of an operating lease rather than a capitalized lease and therefore not adding a liability to the balance sheet and preserving a good borrowing capacity, a good rate of return, current ratio, and ratio of debt to stockholders' equity.[5] The expensing of an operating lease constitutes a good form of "off-balance-sheet financing."

TYPES OF LEASES OF PERSONAL PROPERTY AND CRITERIA FOR CAPITALIZATION

As stated earlier, the lease that transfers substantially all the risks and benefits of ownership is essentially capitalized as an asset by the lessee and a sale by the lessor. FASB No. 13 identified four criteria applicable to both lessor and lessee and two criteria applicable only to the lessee to help in the classification of personal property leases. The capitalization criteria applicable to both lessee and lessor are:

1. The lease transfers ownership of the property to the lessee.
2. There is a bargain purchase option in the lease contract.
3. The lease term is equal to 75 percent of the estimated economic life of the leased property.
4. The present value of the minimum lease payments (excluding executory costs) equals or exceeds 90 percent of the fair value of the leased property of the lessor.[6]

The capitalization criteria applicable to the lessor only are:

1. The collectibility of the minimum lease payments is reasonably predictable.
2. No important uncertainties surrounded the amount of unreimbursable costs yet to be incurred by the lessor under the lease.

Given the above criteria, the classification of the lessee is one of the following:

1. An *operating lease* if the lease does not meet any of the four criteria applicable to both lessee and the lessor.
2. A *capital lease* if the lease meets any of the four criteria applicable to both the lessee and lessor.

The classification by the lessor is one of the following:

1. A *sales-type lease* if (a) the lease meets one or more of the four criteria applicable to both the lessee and lessor, (b) the lease meets both of the criteria applicable to lessor only and, (c) there is a manufacturer's or dealer's profit (or loss) to the lessor mea-

sured by the difference between the fair value of the leased property at the inception of the lease and the lessor's cost or carrying value (book value).

2. A *direct financing lease* if (a) the lease meets one or more of the four criteria applicable to both the lessee and lessor, (b) the lease meets both or all criteria applicable to the lessor only, and (c) there is no manufacturer's or dealer's profit (or loss) to the lessor.

3. An *operating lease* if the lease does not meet any of the four criteria applicable to both lessee and lessor and does not meet both the criteria applicable to the lessor.

ACCOUNTING FOR CAPITAL LEASE BY THE LESSEE

Important Elements of a Capital Lease

The computation and entries required in a capital lease depend on a good understanding of the following four key elements:

1. *Minimum lease payments*: They are the payments accepted or required to be paid by the lessee to the lessor. They include the following:
   A. *Minimum rental payments*, which are the minimum required payments by the lessee under the lease terms.
   B. *Guaranteed residual value*, which is an estimated residual value of the leased property as guaranteed by the lessee or a third party, unrelated to the lessor. It is the amount that the lessor has the right to require the lessee to purchase the asset that the lessor is guaranteed to realize.[7]
   C. *Penalty on failure to renew or extend* the lease that is sometimes required of the lessee.
   D. *Bargain purchase option*, which is an option at the inception of the lease, to purchase the lease property at the end of the lease them at a fixed price sufficiently below the expected fair value to make the purchase reasonably assured.

2. *Executory costs*, which are the ownership-type costs, such as insurance, maintenance, and tax expenses, to be excluded, if borne by the lessee, from the computation of present value of the minimum lease payments.

3. *The discount rate*, which is used in the computation of the present value of the minimum lease payments and included after:

A. *The lessee's incremental borrowing rate*, defined as "the rate that, at inception of the lease, the lessee would have incurred to borrow the funds necessary to buy the leased asset on a secured loan with repayment terms similar to the payment schedule called for in the lease,"[8] or

B. *The lessor's interest rate implicit in the lease* if known by the lessee and it is less than the lessee's incremental borrowing rate. It is the discount rate that equates the present value of the minimum lease payments and any unguaranteed residual value acquiring the lease to the fair value of the leased property to the lessor.[9]

Capital Lease by the Lessee Illustrated

This case is a lease without a purchase or bargain purchase option (annuity due basis). The Zribi (lessor) Company and the Alvertos (lessee) Company sign a lease agreement on January 1, 1996, calling for the Zribi Company to lease restaurant equipment to the Alvertos Company beginning January 1, 1996. The relevant information is as follows:

1. The lease term is five years. The lease is noncancelable and requires equal payments of $14,990.81 at the beginning of each year.

2. The equipment has a fair value and cost of $50,000, estimated life of five years, and a zero residual value.

3. The Alvertos Company agrees to pay the executory costs of $3,000 per year, which is included in the annual payments to the Zribi Company.

4. There are no renewal or purchase options, with the equipment reverting to the Zribi Company.

5. The Alvertos' incremental borrowing rate is 11 percent per year, the Zribi's implicit lease rate is 10 percent and is known to the Alvertos Company.

The lease meets two criteria for a classification as a capital lease—namely, (1) a lease term of five years equal to the equipment's economic life, and (2) a present value of lease payments of $50,000 (assigned

Exhibit 2.1
Alvertos Company: Lease Amortization Schedule (Annuity Due Basis)

Date	Annual Lease Payment (a)	Executory Costs (b)	Interest at 10% on Unpaid Obligations (c)	Reduction of Lease Obligation (d)	Balance of Lease Obligation Liability (e)
1/1/96					$50,000.00
1/1/96	$14,990.81	$3,000	$------0------	$11,990.81	$38,009.19
1/1/97	$14,990.81	$3,000	$3,800.919	$ 8,189.891	$29,819.299
1/1/98	$14,990.81	$3,000	$2,981.929	$ 9,008.881	$20,810.418
1/1/99	$14,990.81	$3,000	$2,081.041	$ 9,909.769	$10,900.700
1/1/00	$14,990.81	$3,000	$1,090.064	$10,900.700	$-----0-----
	$74,954.05	$15,000.00	$9,953.953	$50,000.00	

(a)   Required lease payments

(b)   Executory costs paid by the lessee and included in rental payments

(c)   Columns (e) at the beginning of the year X 10% except for 1/1/96

(d)   (a) - (b) - (c)

(e)   Preceding balance - (d)

below) that is higher than 90 percent of fair value of the equipment ($50,000). The capitalized amount as an asset is the present value of the minimum lease payments. It is computed as follows:

Capitalized amount = ($14,990.81 − $3,000) × 4.16986 (the present value of an annuity due of $1 for 5 periods at 10%) = $11,990.81 × 4.16986 = $50,000.

All the relevant information is computed in Exhibit 2.1. The journal entries are as follows:

1. Recording of the capital lease on January 1, 1996:

Leased Equipment Under Capital
Leases $50,000

    Obligation Under Capital Leases $50,000

The entry recognizes an asset and an obligation at the present value of rental payments ($50,000) rather than the total annual rental payments of $74,954.05 ($14,990.81 × 5).

2. Recording the first rental payment in advance on January 1, 1996:

Property Taxes Expenses	$3,000.00	
Obligations Under Capital Lease	$11,990.81	
Cash		$14,990.81

This entry recognizes (a) the executory costs of $3,000, (b) the principal (or reduction of the lease obligation) or $11,990.81, and (c) zero interest expense since no interest has accrued.

3. Recognition of accrued interest as December 31, 1996:

Interest Expense	$3,800.919	
Accrued Interest on Obligation Under Capital Lease (or Interest Payable)		$3,800.919

The interest expense is recognized in the year it is accrued as a result of the applicable of the accrual concept.

4. Recognition of annual depreciation of leased equipment on December 31, 1996:

Deprecation Expense–Capital Leases	$10,000	
Accumulated Depreciation–Capital Leases		$10,000
($50,000/5 years)		

5. At the end of the year, the Obligation Under Capital Leases on the balance sheet is divided into its current and noncurrent portion as follows:

A. *Current Liabilities*

Interest Payable	$3,800.919
Obligations Under Capital Leases	$8,185.891

B. *Noncurrent Liabilities*

Obligation Under Capital Leases	$29,819.891

Exhibit 2.2
Alvertos Company: Charges to Operations—Capital Lease Versus Operating Lease

					Operating	
		Capital Lease			Lease	Difference
					Charges	
Year	Depreciation	Executory Costs	Interest	Total Charge		
1996	$10,000.00	$3,000.00	$3,800.919	$16,800.919	$14,990.81	$1,810.109
1997	$10,000.00	$3,000.00	$2,981.929	$15,981.929	$14,990.81	$991.119
1998	$10,000.00	$3,000.00	$2,081.041	$15,081.041	$14,990.81	$90.231
1999	$10,000.00	$3,000.00	$1,090.064	$14,090.064	$14,990.81	$(900.746)
2000	$10,000.00	$3,000.00	$-----0-----	$13,000.000	$14,990.81	$(1,990.81)
	$50,000.00	$15,000.00	$9,953.953	$74,954.05	$74,954.05	$----0----

6. Recording the second rental payment in advance January 1, 1997:

Property Tax Expenses	$3,000.000
Accrued Interest on Obligation	
Under Capital Lease	$3,800.919
Obligation Under Capital Lease	$8,189.851
Cash	$14,990.81

7. The same pattern of entries is followed through the year 2000.

Operating Method of the Lessee Illustrated

If the capital lease between the Zribi Company and the Alvertos Company was in fact an operating lease, only the rental payments will be recorded at the beginning of each year as follows:

Rent Expense	$14,990.81
Cash	$14,990.81

No rent asset or corresponding liability is recognized in the balance sheet. Only rent expense is recognized in the income statement, and a note disclosure is required for all operating leases that have noncancelable leases in excess of one year.

A comparison of the charges under the capital lease approach and the operating lease approach, as shown in Exhibit 2.2, indicates that the total charges are the same, and the charges are higher in the earlier years and lower in the later years under a capital lease. The choice of capitalization under capital lease rather than expensing under an operation lease results in:

1. Higher short- and long-term debt because of the recognition of Obligations Under Capital Lease,
2. Higher fixed assets because of the recognition of Leased Equipment Under Capital Leases, and
3. Lower income in the earlier years and higher income in the later years of the life of the lease.

ACCOUNTING FOR LEASES BY THE LESSOR

The lessor's interest in leases is related to the following three benefits:

1. *Interest Revenue*. Leasing is a form of financing, therefore financial institutions and leasing companies find leasing attractive because it provides competitive interest margins.
2. *Tax Incentives*. In many cases, companies that lease cannot use the tax benefit, but leasing provides them with an opportunity to transfer such tax benefits to another party (the lessor) in return for a lower rental rate on the leased asset.
3. *High Residual Value*. Another advantage to the lessor is the reversion of the property at the end of the lease term. Residual values can produce large profits.[10]

As explained earlier, the classification of leases by the lessor results in one of three types of leases: operating, sales-type, or direct financing.

Direct Financing Leases by the Lessor: Key Concepts

As explained earlier, a direct financing lease is one that meets one or more of the criteria applicable to both lessee and lessor, meets both of the criteria applicable to the lessor only, and there is no profit or loss to the lessor. Because there is no profit and loss in a direct financing lease, the net receivable to the lessor must equal the cost of carrying value of the property. Three accounts need to be defined:

1. *Lease Payments Receivable or Minimum Lease Payments Receivable*: This is the gross investment. It is equal to the sum of:
   a.   The undiscounted minimum lease payments to be received by the lessor plus
   b.   The unguaranteed residual value accruing to the lessor.

   Note that:
   a.   The "minimum lease payments" include: (1) rental payments (excludes executory costs), (2) a bargain purchase option (if any), (3) a guaranteed residual value (if any), and (4) penalty for failure to renew (if any).
   b.   The lease payments receivable includes either guaranteed or unguaranteed residual value with the guaranteed residual value included in the minimum lease payments and the unguaranteed residual value included as a second item.

2. *Unearned Interest Revenue or Unearned Interest–Leases*: This is the difference between the gross investment or lease payment receivable and the cost or carrying value of the lease property.

3. *Net Investment to the Lessor*: This is the difference between the gross investment and the unearned interest revenue. Generally the balance sheet treats the unearned interest revenue as a contra account to be deducted from the Minimum Lease Payments Receivable to yield the "net investment to the lessor."

Direct Financing by the Lessor: Illustrated

Returning to the previous example between the Zribi Company and the Alvertos Company, the following information is relevant:

1. The five-year uncancelable lease beginning January 1, 1996, requires equal rental payments of $14,990.81 that include $3,000 of property costs.

2. The equipment has a cost and a fair value of $50,000, an estimated life of five years, and no residual value.

3. No initial direct costs are included and no renewable options are included with the property returning to the Zribi Company at the end of the lease.

4. Collectiblity of payments is assumed and no unreimbursable costs are expected.

5. The interest rate implicit in the lease is 10 percent. It is the rate that, when applied to the gross receivable, will discount that amount to a present value that is equal to the net receivable. The annual rental payments charged to the lessor are computed as follows:

Annual payments: Known Present Value Equal to the Cost of Equipment
Present Value of an Annuity due of $1 for 5 periods at 10 percent

$$= \quad \frac{\$50,000}{4.16986}$$

$$= \quad \$11,990.81$$

6. The lease meets the criteria for a direct financing lease classification. It is a direct financing lease rather than a sales-type lease because the fair value (present value) of the property is equal to its cost.

7. The Lease Payments Receivable is equal to the minimum lease payments minus executory costs paid by the lessor plus the undescended unguaranteed residual value accruing to the lessor. Therefore: Lease Payments Receivable = [($14,990.81 − $3,000) × 5] + $0 = $59,954.05.

8. The Unearned Interest Revenue is equal to the minimum lease payment receivable minus the cost or carrying value of the leased equipment. Therefore: Unearned Interest Revenue = $59.954.05 − 450,000 = $9,954,05.

9. The Net Investment to the lessor is equal to $50,000, the minimum lease payments receivable of $59,954.05 minus the Unearned Interest Revenue of $9,954.05.

10. The accounting entries based on the lease amortization schedule shown in Exhibit 2.3 are as follows:

A. Initial recording of the lease on January 1, 1996:

Lease Payments Receivable	$59,954.05	
Equipment		$50,000
Unearned Interest Revenue– Leases		$9,954.05

Exhibit 2.3
Zribi Company: Lease Amortization Schedule (Annuity Due Basis)

Date	Annual Lease Payment (a)	Executory Costs (b)	Interest on Net Investment at 10% (c)	Net Investment Recovery (d)	Net Investment (e)
1/1/96					$50,000.00
1/1/96	$ 14,990.81	$3,000.00	$-----0-----	$11,990.81	$38,009.19
1/1/97	$ 14,990.81	$3,000.00	$3,800.919	$ 8,189.891	$29,819.299
1/1/98	$ 14,990.81	$3,000.00	$2,981.929	$ 9,008.881	$20,810.418
1/1/99	$ 14,990.81	$3,000.00	$2,081.041	$ 9,909.769	$10,900.700
1/1/00	$ 14,990.81	$3,000.00	$1,090.064	$10,900.700	$-----0-----
	$ 75,954.05	$15,000.00	$9,953.953	$50,000.00	

(a)   Required lease payments producing 10% return on net investment

(b)   Executory costs paid by the lessee and included in the rental payments

(c)   Column (e) at the beginning of the year X 10% (except for 1/1/96)

(d)   (a) - (b) - (c)

(e)   Preceding balance minus (d)

B. Collection of first year's lease payment in January 1, 1996

Cash	$14,990.81	
Lease Payment Receivable		$11,990.81
Property Tax Expense/Property Taxes Payable		$3,000.00

C. Recognition on December 31, 1996, of interest revenue earned during the first year:

Unearned Interest Revenue–Leases	$3,800.919	
Interest Revenue–Leases		$3,800.919

The unearned interest revenue is amortized by the use of the effective interest method. At the end of the year 1996 the lease payments receivable is disclosed as both current and noncurrent assets as follows:

1. The net investment at the end of 1996 is equal to $441,810.109 (the balance of 1/1/96 of $38,009.19 plus the interest receivable for 1996 of $3,800.919).

2. The current portion ($14,990.81) is the net investment to be received in 1997 of $8,189.891 plus the interest of $3,800.919.

3. The noncurrent portion is the $29,819.299 [lease payments] receivable of $35,972.43 ($11,990.81 × 3) minus unearned interest revenue of $6,153.054 ($1,090.064 + $2,081.041 + $2,981.919).

    D. Collection of second year's lease payments:

Cash	$14,990.81	
Lease Payments Receivable		$11,990.81
Property Tax Expense/Payable		$3,000.00

    E. Recognition of December 31, 1997, interest revenue earned during the year:

Unearned Interest Revenue–Leases	$2,981.929	
Interest Revenue–Leases		$2,981.929

    F. The entries should be similar through the year zero.

Operating Method of the Lessor: Illustrated

The lessor using the operating method proceeds by recording every rental payments as a rental revenue, recording a depreciation expense for the leased equipment, and recording other additional costs as expense. Returning to the previous example between the Zrili Company and the Alvertos Company, the following entries are made:

    A. Collection of Rental Payment on Operating Lease on 1/1/96

Cash	$14,990.81	
Rental Revenue		$14,990.81

    B. Recognition of Annual Depreciation expense on 12/31/96

Deprecation Expense–Leased Equipment	$5,000.00	
Accumulate Depreciation–Leased Equipment		$5,000.00

CONCLUSIONS

Accounting for long-term leases involves either expensing or capitalizing the rental expenses. FASB Statement No. 13, which is the main subject of this chapter, outlines explicitly the techniques to be used under specific conditions by the lessee and the lessor. More advanced techniques are examined in Chapter 3.

NOTES

1. "Accounting for Leases," *FASB Statement No. 13 as Amended and Interpreted through January 1990* (Norwalk, Conn.: FASB, 1990), Sec. 1.10.101.

2. John H. Myers, "Reporting of Leases in Financial Statements," *Accounting Research Standard No. 4* (New York: American Institute of Certified Public Accountants, 1964).

3. Yuji, Ijiri, *Recognition of Contractual Rights and Obligations*, Research Report (Stamford, Conn.: FASB, 1980).

4. Donald E. Kieso, and Jerry J. Weygandt, *Intermediate Accounting*, 4th ed. (New York: John Wiley, 1993), p. 1123.

5. E. A., Imhoff, Jr., R. C. Lipe, and D. W. Wright, "Operating Leases: Impact of Constructive Capitalization," *Accounting Horizons* (March 1991).

6. *FASB Statement No. 13*, par. 7.

7. Sometimes the lessee is required to make up a *residual value deficiency* resulting from unusual events. Such deficiency is not included in the minimum lease payments but is recognized as period costs when incurred, as suggested by "Lessee Guarantee of the Residual Value of Leased Property," *FASB Interpretation No. 19* (Stamford, Conn: FASB, 1977), par. 3.

8. *FASB Statement No. 13*, par 5(1).

9. Ibid., par. 5(k).

10. Kieso and Weygandt, *Intermediate Accounting*, p. 1133.

SELECTED READING

"Accounting for Leases." *FASB Statement No. 13 as Amended and Interpreted through January 1990* (Norwalk, Conn: FASB, 1990).

Accounting for Long-Term Leases: Part II

This chapter introduces more advanced techniques for accounting for leases.

IMPACT OF RESIDUAL VALUES

Residual value, which is the estimated fair value of the leased asset at the end of the lease, can be either guaranteed or unguaranteed by the lessee. As stated earlier, guaranteed residual values are included in the minimum lease payments. Both guaranteed and unguaranteed residual values affect accounting by the lessee and lessor. For the lessor the determination of the lease payments with a residual value is also different. For example, let's suppose that the Zribi Company from chapter 2 expected the restaurant equipment to have a residual value of $2,500. It would compute the lease payments as shown in Exhibit 3.1.

The Case of a Guaranteed Residual Value

The guaranteed residual value is included in the minimum lease payments, which require that the lessee capitalizes the present value of the amount guaranteed. To illustrate let's return to the Zribi Company as the lessor and the Alvertos Company as the lessee example and assume that the Alvertos Company agrees to guarantee the entire amount of the residual value of $2,500. The capitalized amount for the Alvertos Company is as follows:

Exhibit 3.1
Zribi's Computation of Lease Payments in the Case of Residual Value
(Lessor's Computation, Annuity Due Basis)

1. Fair Market Value of Equipment of the Zribi Company	$50,000.00
2. Less Present Value of Residual Value ($2,500 X 0.62092)	$ 1,552.30
3. Amount to be Recovered by the Zribi Company	
Through the Lease Payments	$48,447.70
4. Five Periodic Lease Payments ($48,447.70/4.16986)	$11,618.543

1. Present value of five annual rental payments discounted at 10 percent

($11,618.543 × 4.16986) $48,447.70

Plus

2. Present value of a single sum of $2,500 (the guaranteed residual value)

discounted at 10 percent $1,552.30
($2,500 × 0.62092)

3. Present value of minimum lease payments $50,000.00

The Alvertos Company lease amortization schedule is shown in Exhibit 3.2. It is the basis for the following entries:

1. Capitalization of lease on 1/1/96
    Leased Equipment Under Capital
    Leases $50,000
        Obligation Under Capital Leases $50,000
2. First rental payment on 1/1/96
    Property Tax Expense $3,000.00
    Obligations Under Capital Leases $11,618.543
        Cash $14,618.543
3. Recognition of accrued interest on 12/31/96
    Interest Expense $3,838.145
        Interest Payable $3,838.145
        (or Accrued Interest Obligation
        Under Capital Leases)

Exhibit 3.2
Alvertos Company Lease Amortization Schedule (Lessee's Computation, Annuity Due Basis) and Guaranteed Residual Value (GRV)

Date	Lease Payment Plus GRV (a)	Executory Costs (b)	Interest at 10% on Unpaid Obligation (c)	Reduction of Lease Obligation (d)	Balance of Lease Obligation Liability (e)
1/1/96					$50,000.00
1/1/96	$14,618.543	$ 3,000	$----0----	$11,618.543	$38,381.457
1/1/97	$14,618.543	$ 3,000	$ 3,838.145	$ 7,780.398	$30,601.059
1/1/98	$14,618.543	$ 3,000	$ 3,060.105	$ 8,558.438	$22,042.621
1/1/99	$14,618.543	$ 3,000	$ 2,204.262	$ 9,414.281	$12,628.34
1/1/00	$14,618.543	$ 3,000	$ 1,262.834	$10,355.709	$ 2,272.631
12/31/00	$ 2,500.000		$ 227.263	$ 2,272.03*	$-----0-----
	$75,592.715	$15,000	$10,592.609*	$50,000.00*	

*rounded

(a)   Required Lease Payments

(b)   Executory costs paid by the lessee and included in rental payments

(c)   Column (e) at the preceding balance X 10% except for 1/1/96

(d)   (a) - (b) - (c)

(e)   Preceding balance - (d)

4. Recognition of the annual depreciation of leased equipment on 12/31/96

> Depreciation Expense–Capital
> Leases $9,500.00
>
> > Accumulated Depreciation–Cap-
> > ital Leases $9,500.00
>
> [($50,000 − $2,500)/ 5 years]

5. At the end of the year 1996, the Obligation Under Capital Leases in the balance sheet is divided into its current and noncurrent portions as follows:

A. Current Liabilities

Interest Payable	$3,838.145
Obligations Under Capital Leases	$7,780.398

B. Noncurrent Liabilities

Obligations Under Lease	$30,601.059

6. Recording the second rental payments in advance 1/1/97

Property Tax Expense	$3,000.00	
Obligations Under Capital Leases	$7,780.398	
Accrued Interest on Obligations Under Capital Leases	$3,838.398	
Cash		$14,618.543

7. The same patterns of entries are followed through the year zero

The Case of an Unguaranteed Residual Value

The lessee does not recognize the unguaranteed residual value in the computation of the minimum lease payments and the capitalization of the leased asset under obligation. To illustrate, let's return to the Zribi Company as the lessor and the Alvertos Company as the lessee example and assume that the Alvertos Company does not agree to guarantee the entire amount of the residual value of $2,500. The capitalized amount for the Alvertos Company is as follows:

1. Present value of five annual rental payments discounted at 10 percent

($11,681.543 × 4.16986) $48,447.70

Plus

2. Unguaranteed residual value of $2,500 not capitalized

$----0----
_____

3. Present value of minimum lease payments

$48,447.70

The Alvertos Company lease amortization schedule is shown in Exhibit 3.3. It is the basis for the following entries:

Exhibit 3.3
Alvertos Company Lease Amortization Schedule (Lessee's Computation, Annuity Due Basis) and Unguaranteed Residual Value

Date	Lease Payments (a)	Executory Costs (b)	Interest at 10% on Unpaid Obligations (c)	Reduction of Lease Obligation (d)	Balance of Lease Obligation Liability (e)
1/1/96					$48,447.70
1/1/96	$14,618.543	$3,000	$-----0-----	$11,618.543	$36,829.152
1/1/97	$14,618.543	$3,000	$3,682.915	$ 7,935.628	$28,893.529
1/1/98	$14,618.543	$3,000	$2,889.352	$ 8,729.191	$20,164.338
1/1/99	$14,618.543	$3,000	$2,016.433	$ 9,602.11	$10,562.228
1/1/00	$14,618.543	$3,000	$1,056.222	$10,562.22*	$-----0-----
	$73,092.715	$15,000	$ 9,644.922	$48,447.70*	

*Rounding error

1. Capitalization of lease on 1/1/96

Leased Equipment Under Capital Leases	$48,447.70	
Obligations Under Capital Leases		$48,447.70

2. First rental payment on 1/1/96

Property Tax Expense	$3,000.00	
Obligations Under Capital Leases	$11,618.543	
Cash		$14,618.543

3. Recognition of accrued interest on 12/31/96

Interest Expense	$3,682.915	
Interest Payable		$3,682.915

4. Recognition of annual depreciation expense on 12/31/96

Depreciation Expense-Capital Leases	$9,689.54	
Accumulated depreciation- Capital Leases		$9,689.54
($48,447.70/5 years)		

5. At the end of the year 1996 the Obligation Under Capital Leases in the balance sheet is divided into its current and noncurrent portions as follows:

A. Current Liabilities

Interest Payable	$3,682.915
Obligations Under Capital Leases	$7,935.628

B. Noncurrent Liabilities

Obligation Under Capital Leases	$28,893.529

6. Recording the second rental payment on 1/1/97

Property Tax Expense	$3,000.00
Obligations Under Capital Leases	$3,682.915
Accrued Interest on Obligations Under Capital Leases	$7,935.628
Cash	$14,618.543

7. The same patterns of entries are followed through the year zero.

The Case of a Residual Value for the Lessor

For the lessor the assumption is that the residual value will be realized whether it is guaranteed or unguaranteed. Returning to the previous example of the Zribi Company as the lessor and the Alvertos Company as the lessee and the residual value of $2,500 (whether guaranteed or unguaranteed), the following information is relevant to the lessor.

1. Gross Investment: ($11,618.543 × 5) + $2,500 = $60,592.715
2. Unearned Interest Revenue: $60,592.715 − $50,000 = $10,592.715
3. Net Investment = $60,592.715 − $10,592.715 = $50,000.00

The lease amortization schedule for the lessor is illustrated in Exhibit 3.4. It is the basis of the following entries:

1. Initial recording of the lease at its inception on 1/1/96

Lease Payments Receivable	$60,592.715

Exhibit 3.4
Zribi Company Lease Amortization Schedule (Lessor's Computation, Annuity Due Basis) and Guaranteed Residual Value

Date	Lease Payment Plus GRV (a)	Executory Costs (b)	Interest at 10% on Net Investment (c)	Net Investment Recovery (d)	Net Investment
1/1/96					$50,000.00
1/1/96	$14,818.543	$3,000	$-----0-----	$11,618.543	$38,381.457
1/1/97	$14,818.543	$3,000	$ 3,838.145	$ 7,780.398	$30,601.059
1/1/98	$14,818.543	$3,000	$ 3,060.105	$ 8,558,438	$22,042.621
1/1/99	$14,818.543	$3,000	$ 2,204.262	$ 9,414.281	$12,628.34
1/1/00	$14,818.543	$3,000	$ 1,262.834	$10,355.709	$ 2,272.631
12/31/00	$ 2,500.00	$3,000	$ 227.263	$ 2,272.03*	$-----0----
	$75,592.715	$15,000	$10,592.609*	$50,000.00*	

*rounded

(a)   Required Lease Payments

(b)   Executory Costs paid by the lessee and included in rental payments

(c)   Column (e) at the preceding balance X 10% except for 1/1/96

(d)   (a) - (b) - (c)

(e)   Preceding balance - (d)

Equipment	$50,000.00
Unearned Interest Revenue- Leases	$10,592.715

2. Recording of first rental payment on 1/1/96

Cash	$14,618.543	
Lease Payments Receivable		$11,618.543
Property Tax Expense/Property Tax Payable		$3,000.00

3. Recognition of accrued interest on 12/31/96

| Unearned Interest Revenue–Leases | $3,838.145 | |
| Interest Revenue–Leases | | $3,838.145 |

SALES-TYPE LEASES: ACCOUNTING FOR THE LESSOR

The major difference between a direct financing lease and a sales-type lease is the presence of a manufacturer's or dealer's profit or loss in a sales-type lease and the accounting for initial direct costs. This profit or loss is equal to the difference between:

1. The present value of the minimum lease payments (net of executory costs) computed at the interest rate implicit in the lease (i.e., the sales price), and
2. The cost or carrying value of the asset plus any initial direct costs less the present value of the unguaranteed residual value accruing to the benefit of the lessor.

To illustrate a sales-type lease, let's assume the same example as in direct financing where (1) the residual value is $2,500 (with a present value of $1,553.30), (2) the equipment had a cost of $40,000 to the lessor, the Zribi Company, and (3) the fair market value of the residual value is $1,000.

A. The following information is relevant to the lessor in case the residual value is a guaranteed residual value:
1. Gross Investment: ($11,618.543 × 5) + $2,500 = $60,592.715
2. Unearned Interest Revenue: $60,592.715 − $50,000 = $10,592.715
3. Sale Price of the Asset: ($48,447.70 + 1,552.30) = $50,000.00
4. Cost of Good Sold: $40,000
5. Gross Profit: ($50,000 − $40,000) = $10,000

B. The following information is relevant to the lessor in case of an unguaranteed residual value:
1. Gross Investment: ($11,618,543 × 5) + $2,500 = $60,592.715
2. Unearned Interest Revenue: $60,592.715 − $50,000 = $10,592.715
3. Sale Price of the Asset: $48,447.70
4. Cost of Goods Sold: $40,000 − $1,552.30 = $38,447.70
5. Gross Profit: ($48,447.70 − $38,447.70) = $10,000.00

C. The entries assuming guaranteed residual value are:

1. Initial recording of the sales-type lease on 1/1/96

Minimum Lease Receivable	$60,592.715	
Cost of Goods Sold	$40,000.00	
Sales Revenue		$50,000.00
Equipment Held for Lease		$40,000.00
Unearned Interest Leases		$10,592.715

2. Collection of annual payment of the 1/1/96

Cash	$14,618.543	
Minimum Lease Receivable		$11,618.543
Property Expense/Payable		$3,000.00

3. Recognition of interest revenue on 12/31/96

Unearned Interest–Leases	$3,682.915	
Interest Revenue		$3,682.915

4. Collection of second annual payment for 1/1/97

Cash	$14,618.543	
Minimum Lease Receivable		$11,618.543
Property Expenses/ Payable		$3,000.000

5. Recognition of interest revenue as of 12/31/97

Unearned Interest–Leases	$2,889.352	
Interest Revenue		$2,889.352

6. Recognition of residual value at the end of lease term (12/31/00)

Equipment	$1,000.00	
Cash	$1,500.00	
Lease Payment Receivable		$2,500.00

D. The entries assuming an unguaranteed residual value are:

1. Initial recording of the sales-type lease on 1/1/96

Minimum Lease Receivable	$60,592.715	
Cost of Goods Sold	$38,447.70	
Sales Revenue		$48,447.70
Equipment		$40,000.00
Unearned Interest Revenue		$10,592.715

2. Collection of annual payment for 1/1/96

Cash	$14,618.543	
Minimum Lease Receivable		$11,618.543
Property Tax Expense/ Payable		$3,000.000

3. Recognition of interest revenue on 12/31/96

Unearned Interest-Leases	$3,682.915	
Interest Revenue		$3,682.915

4. Collection of second annual payment for 1/1/97

Cash	$14,618.543	
Minimum Lease Receivable		$11,618.543
Property Tax Expense/ Payable		$3,000.000

5. Recognition of interest revenue on 12/31/97

Unearned Interest-Leases	$2,889.352	
Interest Revenue		$2,889.352

6. Recognition of residual value at the end of the lease term (12/31/00)

Equipment	$1,000.00	
Cash	$1,500.00	
Lease Payment Receivable		$2,500.00

ACCOUNTING FOR INITIAL DIRECT COSTS BY THE LESSOR

Initial direct costs have been redefined in FASB Statement No. 91.[1] Basically the initial direct costs of a lease transaction include two types as follows:

1. Incremental direct costs are the costs resulting from and are essential to the lease transaction.
2. Internal direct costs are the costs related to the evaluation of the lessee's personal condition, and other costs of the activities performed by the lessor.

The accounting treatment for initial direct costs is different for each type of lease:

1. For an operating lease, the initial direct costs are recorded as prepaid assets and allocated over the lease term as an expense proportionally to the rental receipts.
2. For a direct financing lease, the initial direct costs are deferred and added to the net investment in the leases and amortized over the life of the lease as a yield adjustment.
3. For a sales-type lease, the initial direct costs are expensed in the same period.

ACCOUNTING FOR SALE-LEASEBACK

A sale-leaseback occurs when the owner of the asset sells the asset to another and simultaneously leases it back from the buyer (1) to benefit from better financing and (2) to derive a tax advantage from deducting the entire lease payment. Two situations are possible:

1. If the lease meets the condition for a capital lease, the profit from the transaction is deferred and amortized over the lease term by the lessee in proportion to the amortization of the leased asset.
2. If the lease does not meet the conditions for a capital lease, it is considered an operating lease and the profit is amortized proportionally to the rental payments.

Exhibit 3.5
Lessee's Lease Amortization Schedule

Date	Annual Rental Payment	Interest at 10%	Reduction of Balance	Balance
1/1/96				$10,460,000
1/1/96	$3,000,000.00	$-----0-----	$3,000,000	$ 7,460,000
1/1/97	$3,000,000.00	$746,000	$2,254,000	$ 5,206,000
1/1/98	$3,000,000.00	$520,000	$2,480,000	$ 2,726,000
1/1/99	$3,000,000.00	$272,000	$2,726,000	$-----0-----

Any loss, however, is recognized immediately. To illustrate a sale-leaseback transaction, assume that the Lessee Corporation, on January 1, 1996, sells a ship having a book value of $2,460,000 to the Lessor Corporation for $10,460,000 and simultaneously leases it back under the following conditions:

1. The term of the lease is four years, noncancelable.
2. The payments at the beginning of every year are $3,000,000.
3. The fair value of the ship is $10,460,000 on 1/1/96 with a four-year economic life.
4. The lessor's rate is 10 percent.

Assuming the lease is a capital lease, the entries based on Exhibit 3.5 are as follows:

1. Sale of ship by the lessee to the lessor on 1/1/96

Cash	$10,460,000	
Ship		$2,460,000
Unearned Profit on Sale-Leaseback		$8,000,000

2. Initial recording of sale-leaseback on 1/1/96

Leased Ship Under Capital Leases	$10,460,000	
Obligations Under Capital Leases		$10,460,000

3. Recording of first lease payment on 1/1/96

Obligations Under Capital Leases	$3,000,000	
Cash		$3,000,000

4. Recording of depreciation expense on 12/31/96

Depreciation Expense	$2,615,000	
Accumulated Depreciation		$2,615,000
($10,460,000/4)		

5. Amortization of unearned profit on sales-leaseback on 12/31/96

Unearned Profit on Sale-Leaseback	$2,000,000	
Realized Profit on Sale-Leaseback		$2,000,000
(or Depreciation Expense–Leased Ships)		
($8,000,000/4)		

6. Recognition of interest expense on 12/31/96

Interest Expense	$746,000	
Interest Payable		$746,000

To the lessor the entries are as follows on 1/1/96

1.

Ship	$10,460,000	
Cash		$10,460,000

2.

Lease Payments Receivable ($3,000,000 × 4)		$12,000,000
Ship		
Unearned Interest Revenue		

3.

Cash	$3,000,000	
Lease Payments Receivable		$3,000,000

ACCOUNTING FOR LEASES INVOLVING REAL ESTATE

There are specific issues for accounting for leases involving real estate that include lease of land only, lease of both land and buildings, and lease of real estate and equipment.

1. If the lease involves land only, the lease for the lessee is a capital lease if (a) there is a transfer of ownership, and (b) there is a bargain

purchase option, otherwise it is an operating lease. For the lessor the lease is either a sale-type or a direct financing lease if it meets the ownership conditions, the bargain purchase option conditions, and the collectibility and uncertainty tests. Otherwise it is an operating lease.

2. If the lease involves both land and buildings and meets the ownership conditions and the bargain purchase option conditions, it is a capital lease for the lessee and either a sale-type lease or a direct financing lease for the lessor, depending on the existence of a profit or loss.

3. If the lease involves both land and buildings, does not meet the ownership conditions, the bargain purchase option conditions, and the fair value of the land is less than 25 percent of the fair value of both land and buildings, the land portion is ignored and the lease is classified on the basis of the buildings' characteristics.

4. If the lease involves both land and buildings, does not meet the ownership condition and the bargain purchase option condition, and the fair value of the land is more than 25 percent of the fair value of both land and buildings, both the lessee and the lessor account for the land as an operating lease and the buildings as a capital lease if it meets the necessary requirements.

5. If the lease involves both real estate and equipment, the portion of the minimum lease payments applicable to the equipment portion of the lease should be estimated by whatever means are appropriate. The classification of the equipment is done separately from the real estate. The accounting for the real estate portion proceeds as described in the preceding section. For a leased property that is part of a large building, reasonable estimates of the lease property's fair value might be objectively determined by referring to an independent appraisal of the lease property or to estimated replacement cost information.

LEVERAGED LEASES

Definition of Leveraged Leases

The use of leveraged leases for the financing of capital equipment has reached an annual value of $6.5 billion. The leveraged lease allows a boost to the tax benefits to the lessor, who has to come up with a small percentage of the purchase price and finance the rest while keeping 100 percent of the ownership of the asset.

A leveraged lease is defined as one having all of the following characteristics:

1. It meets the definition of a direct financing lease while the 90 percent of fair value criterion does not apply.
2. It involves at least three parties:
   a. Owner-lessor (commonly called equity participant)
   b. A lessee (commonly called user of the asset)
   c. A long-term creditor (commonly called debt participant)
3. The amount of the financing is sufficient to provide the lessor with a substantial "leverage" in the transaction.
4. The leverage debt provided by the long-term creditor (60 percent to 80 percent) is nonrecourse as to the general credit of the lessor. It is secured by the lessee's payment and a security interest in the property. Therefore, the interest rate depends on the credit rating of the lessee rather than the lessor.
5. The lessor buys the asset from the manufacturer using his capital and the capital provided by the long-term creditor. He or she leases the asset to the lessee. The lessor uses the lease payments to make debt service payments (interest and principal) and keeps the remaining difference. The lessor benefits from (a) the lease payments, and (b) the income tax deductions from accelerated depreciating expenses, interest expenses, and other possible expenses. In general, the lessor's net investment declines during the early years once the investment has been completed and rises during the later years of the lease before its final elimination.

Accounting for Leveraged Leases

The lessee should treat the leveraged lease in the same manner as a nonleveraged lease. The lessor's treatment is more complex. The lessor records the investment in the leveraged lease net of the nonrecourse debt. The net of the balances of the following accounts represent the initial and continuing investment in leveraged leases.

A. Rentals receivable, net of that portion of the rental applicable to the principal and interest on the nonrecourse debt.

B. A receivable for the amount of the investment tax credit to be realized on the transaction.

C. The estimated residual value of the leased asset.

D. Unearned and deferred income consisting of (i) the estimated pretax lease income (or loss), after deducting initial direct costs, remaining to be allocated to income over the lease term and (ii) the investment tax credit remaining to be allocated to income over the lease term.

    The investment in leveraged leases less deferred taxes arising from differences between pretax accounting income and taxable income shall represent the lessor's net investment in leveraged leases for purposes of computing periodic net income from the lease.[2]

To illustrate the accounting for leveraged leases, let's consider the following example. The lessor company and lessee company sign a lease agreement dated January 1, 1975, that calls for the lessor company to lease equipment to the lessee company until the beginning of January 1, 1990. The terms and provisions of the lease agreements and other pertinent data are as follows:

Cost of leased asset (equipment)	$1,000,000
Lease term	15 years, dating from January 1, 1975
Lease rental payments	$90,000 per year (payable last day of each year)
Residual value	$200,000 estimated to be realized one year after lease termination. In the eleventh year of the lease the estimate is reduced to $120,000.

Financing:

Equity investment by lessor	$400,000
Long-term nonrecourse debt	$600,000, bearing interest at 9 percent and repayable in annual installments (on last day of each year) of $74,435.30.

Depreciation allowable to lessor for income tax purposes	Seven-year ADR life using double-declining balance method for the first two years (with the half-year convention election applied in the first year) and sum-of-years digits method for remaining life, depreciated to $100,000 salvage value.
Lessor's income tax rate (federal and state)	50.4 percent (assumed to continue in existence throughout the term of the lease)
Investment tax credit	10 percent of equipment cost or $100,000 (realized by the lessor on last day of first year of lease)
Initial direct costs	For simplicity, initial direct costs have not been included in the illustration.

Given the above terms and provisions, the cash flow analysis by years and the allocation of annual cash flow to investment and income are presented in Exhibits 3.6 and 3.7. The journal entries for lessor's initial investment and first year of operations are as follows:

JOURNAL ENTRIES FOR YEAR ENDING DECEMBER 31, 1975

LESSOR'S INITIAL INVESTMENT

Rentals receivable (Exhibit 3.6, total of column 1 less residual value, less totals of columns 3 and 6)	$233,470	
Investment tax credit receivable (Exhibit 3.6 column 7)	$100,000	
Estimated residual value (given)	$200,000	
Unearned and deferred income (Exhibit 3.7, totals of columns 5 and 7)		$133,470
Cash		$400,000
First Year Operation		
Cash	$15,565	

Exhibit 3.6
Cash Flow Analysis by Years

Year	1 Gross lease rentals and residual value	2 Depreciation (for income tax purposes)	3 Loan interest payments	4 Taxable income (loss) (col. 1 − 2 − 3)	5 Income tax credits (charges) (col. 4 × 50.4%)	6 Loan principal payments	7 Investment tax credit realized	8 Annual cash flow (col. 1 − 3 + 5 − 6 + 7)	9 Cumulative cash flow
Initial investment	—	—	—	—	—	—	—	$(400,000)	(400,000)
1	$ 90,000	$ 142,857	$ 54,000	$(106,857)	$ 53,856	$ 20,435	$100,000	169,421	(230,579)
2	90,000	244,898	52,161	(207,059)	104,358	22,274	—	119,923	(110,656)
3	90,000	187,075	50,156	(147,231)	74,204	24,279	—	89,769	(20,887)
4	90,000	153,061	47,971	(111,032)	55,960	26,464	—	71,525	50,638
5	90,000	119,048	45,589	(74,637)	37,617	28,846	—	53,182	103,820
6	90,000	53,061	42,993	(6,054)	3,051	31,442	—	18,616	122,436
7	90,000	—	40,163	49,837	(25,118)	34,272	—	(9,553)	112,883
8	90,000	—	37,079	52,921	(26,672)	37,357	—	(11,108)	101,775
9	90,000	—	33,717	56,283	(28,367)	40,719	—	(12,803)	88,972
10	90,000	—	30,052	59,948	(30,214)	44,383	—	(14,649)	74,323
11	90,000	—	26,058	63,942	(32,227)	48,378	—	(16,663)	57,660
12	90,000	—	21,704	68,296	(34,421)	52,732	—	(18,857)	38,803
13	90,000	—	16,957	73,043	(36,813)	57,478	—	(21,248)	17,555
14	90,000	—	11,785	78,215	(39,420)	62,651	—	(23,856)	(6,301)
15	90,000	—	6,145	83,855	(42,263)	68,290	—	(26,698)	(32,999)
16	200,000	100,000	—	100,000	(50,400)	—	—	149,600	116,601
Totals	$1,550,000	$1,000,000	$516,530	$ 33,470	$(16,869)	$600,000	$100,000	$116,601	

Source: "Accounting for Leases," *FASB Statement No. 13 as Amended and Interpreted Through May 1980* (Stamford, Conn: FASB, 1980), Schedule 2. Reprinted with permission.

Exhibit 3.7
Allocation of Annual Cash Flow to Investment and Income

Year	1 Lessor's net investment at beginning of year	2 Total (from Schedule 2, col. 8)	3 Allocated to investment	4 Allocated to income[1]	5 Pretax income	6 Tax effect of pretax income	7 Investment tax credit
		Annual Cash Flow			Components of Income[2]		
1	$400,000	$169,421	$134,833	$34,588	$9,929	$(5,004)	$29,663
2	265,167	119,923	96,994	22,929	6,582	(3,317)	19,664
3	168,173	89,769	75,227	14,542	4,174	(2,104)	12,472
4	92,946	71,525	63,488	8,037	2,307	(1,163)	6,893
5	29,458	53,182	50,635	2,547	731	(368)	2,184
6	(21,177)	18,616	18,616	—	—	—	—
7	(39,793)	(9,553)	(9,553)	—	—	—	—
8	(30,240)	(11,108)	(11,108)	—	—	—	—
9	(19,132)	(12,803)	(12,803)	—	—	—	—
10	(6,329)	(14,649)	(14,649)	—	—	—	—
11	8,320	(16,663)	(17,382)	719	206	(104)	617
12	25,702	(18,857)	(21,079)	2,222	637	(321)	1,906
13	46,781	(21,248)	(25,293)	4,045	1,161	(585)	3,469
14	72,074	(23,856)	(30,088)	6,232	1,789	(902)	5,345
15	102,162	(26,698)	(35,532)	8,834	2,536	(1,278)	7,576
16	137,694	149,600	137,694	11,906	3,418	(1,723)	10,211
Totals		$516,601	$400,000	$116,601	$33,470	$(16,869)	$100,000

[1]Lease income is recognized as 8.647% of the unrecovered investment at the beginning of each year in which the net investment is positive. The rate is that rate which when applied to the net investment in the years in which the net investment is positive will distribute the net income (net cash flow) to those years. The rate for allocation used in this Schedule is calculated by a trial and error process. The allocation is calculated based upon an initial estimate of the rate as a starting point. If the total thus allocated to income (column 4) differs under the estimated rate from the net cash flow (Schedule 2, column 8) the estimated rate is increased or decreased, as appropriate, to derive a revised allocation. This process is repeated until a rate is selected which develops a total amount allocated to income that is precisely equal to the net cash flow. As a practical matter, a computer program is used to calculate Schedule 3 under successive iterations until the correct rate is determined.

[2]Each component is allocated among the years of positive net investment in proportion to the allocation of net income in column 4.

Source: "Accounting for Leases," *FASB Statement No. 13 as Amended and Interpreted Through May 1980* (Stamford, Conn: FASB, 1980), Schedule 3. Reprinted with permission.

Rentals receivable (Exhibit 3.6, column 1 less columns 3 and 6)		$15,565

(Collection of 1st year's net rental)

Cash*	$100,000	
Investment tax credit receivable (Exhibit 3.6, column 7)		$100,000

(Receipt of investment tax credit)

Unearned and deferred income	$9,929	
Income from leveraged leases (Exhibit 3.7, column 50)		$9,929

(Recognition of first year's portion of pretax income allocated in the same proportion as the allocation of total income $[34,588/116,601] \times 33,470 = 9,929$)

Unearned and deferred income	$29,663	
Investment tax credit recognized (Exhibit 3.7, column 7)		$29,663

(Recognition of first year's portion of investment tax credit allocation in the same proportion as the allocation of total income $[34,588/116,601] \times 100,000 = 29,663$)

Cash (Exhibit 3.6, column 5)	$53,856	
Income tax expense (Exhibit 3.7, column 6)	$5,004	
Deferred taxes		$58,860

To record receipt of first year's tax credit from lease operation, to charge income tax expense for tax effect of pretax accounting income, and to recognize as deferred taxes the tax effect of the difference between pretax accounting income and the tax loss for the year, calculated as follows:

---

*Receipts of the investment tax credit and other tax benefits are shown as cash receipts for simplicity only. Those receipts probably would not be in the form of immediate cash inflow. Instead, they likely would be in the form of reduced payments of taxes on other entities whose operations are joined with the lessor's operations in a consolidated tax return.

Tax loss (Exhibit 3.6 column 4)	$(106,857)
Pretax accounting income	9,929
Difference	$(116.786)
Deferred taxes ($116,786 × 50.4%)	$58,860

The financial statements including the footnotes at the end of the year are as follows:

1. BALANCE SHEET

ASSETS			LIABILITIES		
	December 31,			*December 31,*	
	1976	1975		1976	1975
Investment in leveraged leases	$334,708	$324,207	Deferred taxes arising from leveraged leases	$58,860	$166,535

2. INCOME STATEMENT

(ignoring all income and expense items other than
those relating to leveraged leasing)

	1976	1975
Income from leveraged leases	$ 6,582	$ 9,929
Income before taxes and investment tax credit	6,582	9,929
Less: Income tax expense*	(3,317)	(5,004)
	3,265	4,925
Investment tax credit recognized*	19,664	29,663
Net Income	$22,929	$34,588

3. FOOTNOTES

Investment in Leveraged Leases

The Company is the lessor in a leveraged lease agreement entered into in 1975 under which mining equipment having an estimated economic

---

*These two items may be netted for purposes of presentation in the income statement, provided that the separate amounts are disclosed in a note to the financial statements.

life of 18 years was leased for a term of 15 years. The Company's equity investment represented 40 percent of the purchase price; the remaining 60 percent was furnished by third-party financing in the form of long-term debt that provides for no recourse against property. At the end of the lease term, the equipment is turned back to the Company. The residual value at that time is estimated to be 20 percent of cost. For federal income tax purposes, the company receives the investment tax credit and has the benefit of tax deductions for depreciation on the entire leased asset and for interest on the long-term debt. Since during the early years of the lease those deductions exceed the lease rental income, substantial excess deductions are available to be applied against the company's other income. In the later years of the lease, rental income will excess the deductions and taxes will be payable. Deferred taxes are provided to reflect this reversal. The company's net investment in leveraged lease is composed of the following elements:

| | December 31, | |
	1976	1975
Rentals receivable (net of principal and interest on the nonrecourse debt)	$202,340	$217,905
Estimated residual value of leased assets	200,000	200,000
Less: Unearned and deferred income	(67,632)	(93,878)
Investment in leveraged leases	334,708	324,027
Less: Deferred taxes arising from leveraged leases	(166,535)	(58,860)
Net investment in leveraged leases	$168,173	$265,167

If we assume a revision in the estimated residual value of the leased asset in the eleventh year of the lease from $200,00 to $120,000, then the revised allocation of annual cash flow to investment and income, the balance in investment accounts at the beginning of the eleventh year before revised estimate, and the adjustments of investment of accounts will be as in Exhibits 3.8, 3.9, and 3.10. Finally, the journal entries will be as follows:

Exhibit 3.8
Allocation of Annual Cash Flow to Investment and Income, Revised to Include New Residual Value Estimate

	1	2	3	4	5	6	7
		Annual Cash Flow			Components of Income		
Year	Lessor's net investment at beginning of year	Total	Allocated to investment	Allocated to income[1]	Pretax loss	Tax effect of pretax loss	Investment tax credit
1	$400,000	$169,421	$142,458	$26,963	$(16,309)	$ 8,220	$ 35,052
2	257,542	119,923	102,563	17,360	(10,501)	5,293	22,568
3	154,979	89,769	79,323	10,446	(6,319)	3,184	13,581
4	75,656	71,525	66,425	5,100	(3,085)	1,555	6,630
5	9,231	53,182	52,560	622	(377)	190	809
6	(43,329)	18,616	18,616	—	—	—	—
7	(61,945)	(9,553)	(9,553)	—	—	—	—
8	(52,392)	(11,108)	(11,108)	—	—	—	—
9	(41,284)	(12,803)	(12,803)	—	—	—	—
10	(28,481)	(14,649)	(14,649)	—	—	—	—
11	(13,832)	(16,663)	(16,663)	—	—	—	—
12	2,831	(18,857)	(19,048)	191	(115)	58	248
13	21,879	(21,248)	(22,723)	1,475	(892)	450	1,917
14	44,602	(23,856)	(26,862)	3,006	(1,819)	916	3,909
15	71,464	(26,698)	(31,515)	4,817	(2,914)	1,469	6,262
16	102,979	109,920	102,979	6,941	(4,199)	2,116	9,024
Totals		$476,921	$400,000	$76,921	$(46,530)	$23,451	$100,000

[1]The revised allocation rate is 6.741%.

Source: "Accounting for Leases," *FASB Statement No. 13 as Amended and Interpreted Through May 1980* (Stamford, Conn: FASB, 1980), Schedule 5. Reprinted with permission.

Exhibit 3.9
Balances in Investment Accounts Before Revised Estimate of Residual Value

	1	2	3	4	5	6	7
				Unearned & Deferred Income			
	Rentals receivable[1]	Estimated residual value	Investment tax credit receivable	Pretax income (loss)[2]	Investment tax credit[3]	Deferred taxes[4]	Net investment (col. 1+2+3) less (col. 4+5+6)
Initial investment	$233,470	$200,000	$100,000	$33,470	$100,000	$ —	$400,000
Changes in year of operation							
1	(15,565)	—	(100,000)	(9,929)	(29,663)	58,860	(134,833)
2	(15,565)	—	—	(6,582)	(19,664)	107,675	(96,994)
3	(15,565)	—	—	(4,174)	(12,472)	76,308	(75,227)
4	(15,565)	—	—	(2,307)	(6,893)	57,123	(63,488)
5	(15,565)	—	—	(731)	(2,184)	37,985	(50,635)
6	(15,565)	—	—	—	—	3,051	(18,616)
7	(15,565)	—	—	—	—	(25,118)	9,553
8	(15,564)	—	—	—	—	(26,672)	11,108
9	(15,564)	—	—	—	—	(28,367)	12,803
10	(15,565)	—	—	—	—	(30,214)	14,649
Balances, beginning of eleventh year	$ 77,822	$200,000	$ —	$ 9,747	$ 29,124	$230,631	$ 8,320

[1] Schedule 2, column 1, excluding residual value, less columns 3 and 6.

[2] Schedule 3, column 5.

[3] Schedule 3, column 7.

[4] 50.4% of difference between taxable income (loss), Schedule 2, column 4, and pretax accounting income (loss), Schedule 3, column 5.

Source: "Accounting for Leases," *FASB Statement No. 13 as Amended and Interpreted Through May 1980* (Stamford, Conn: FASB, 1980), Schedule 6. Reprinted with permission.

Exhibit 3.10

Adjustment of Investment Accounts for Revised Estimates of Residual Value in the Eleventh Year

	1	2	3	4	5	6
			Unearned & Deferred Income			Net investment
	Rentals receivable	Estimated residual value	Pretax income (loss)	Investment tax credit	Deferred taxes	(col. 1 + 2) less (col. 3 + 4 + 5)
Balances, beginning of eleventh year (Schedule 6)	$77,822	$200,000	$ 9,747	$29,124	$230,631	$ 8,320
Adjustment of estimated residual value and unearned and deferred income (Schedule 7 – journal entry 1)	—	(80,000)	(19,686)	(7,764)	—	(52,550)
Adjustment of deferred taxes for the cumulative effect on pretax accounting income (Schedule 7 – journal entry 2)	—	—	—	—	(30,398)	30,398
Adjusted balances, beginning of eleventh year	$77,822	$120,000	$ (9,939)	$21,360	$200,233	$(13,832)[1]

[1] Schedule 5, column 1.

Source: "Accounting for Leases," *FASB Statement No. 13 as Amended and Interpreted Through May 1980* (Stamford, Conn: FASB, 1980), Schedule 8. Reprinted with permission.

JOURNAL ENTRIES—REDUCTION IN RESIDUAL VALUE IN ELEVENTH YEAR

1. JOURNAL ENTRY 1

Pretax income (or loss)		$60,314
Unearned and deferred income		$27,450
Pretax income (loss):		
Balance at end of 10th year	$9,747[1]	
Revised balance	$(9,939)[2]	
Adjustment	$(19,686)	
Deferred investment tax credit:		
Balance at end of 10th year	$29,124[3]	
Revised balance	$21,360[4]	
Adjustment	$(7,764)	
Investment tax credit recognized		$7,764
Estimated residual value		$80,000

To record:

(i) The cumulative effect on pretax income and the effect on future income resulting from the decrease in estimated residual value:

Reduction in estimated residual value	$80,000
Less: portion attributed to future years (unearned and deferred income)	$(19,686)
Cumulative effect (charged against current income)	$60,314

(ii) The cumulative and future effect of the change in allocation of the investment tax credit resulting from the reduction in estimated residual value.

[1]Exhibit 3.9, column 4
[2]Exhibit 3.8, total of column 5 less amounts applicable to the first 10 years.
[3]Exhibit 3.9, column 5.
[4]Exhibit 3.8, total of column 7 less amounts applicable to the first 10 years.

2. JOURNAL ENTRY 2

Deferred taxes	$30,398	
Income tax expense		$30,398

To recognize deferred taxes for the difference between pretax accounting income (or loss) and taxable income (or loss) for the effect of the reduction in estimated residual value.

Pretax accounting loss per journal entry 1	($60,314)
Tax income (or loss)	————
Difference	$(60,314)
Deferred taxes ($60,314 × 50.4%)	$(30,398)

NOTES

1. "Accounting for Nonrefundable Fees and Costs Associated with Originating or Acquiring Loans and Initial Direct Costs of Leases," *Statement of Financial Accounting Standards No. 91* (Stamford, Conn.: FASB, 1987).

2. "Accounting for Leases," *FASB Statement No. 13 as Amended and Interpreted Through May 1980* (Stamford, Conn.: FASB, 1980), par. 43.

SELECTED READING

"Accounting for Leases." *FASB Statement No. 13 as Amended and Interpreted Through January 1990* (Norwalk, Conn: FASB, 1990)

4

Issues in Accounting for Long-Term Leases

INTRODUCTION

Accounting for leases is very controversial because of the availability of different alternatives, including capitalization or expensing. Either one of them can be achieved by designing the leasing contract to include covenants permitting one of the alternatives. Therefore if firms attempt to escape the capitalization alternative and opt for the operating one, the user is left with the task of reconstructing the balance sheet to determine the new capital structure as if the firm had adopted the capitalizing alternative. In addition, the capitalizing alternative creates economic consequences and data with potential predictive ability. Accordingly, this chapter examines these issues as a way of assessing the merits of capitalization versus expensing.

LEASE ACCOUNTING RULES

Accounting for leases has always been a controversial accounting issue examined by various standard-setting bodies. The first effort started by the Committee on Accounting Procedures resulted in the publication of the *Accounting Research Bulletin* No. 38, *Disclosure of Long-Term Leases in Financial Statement of Lessees* in 1949. This publication was followed by a second effort of the Accounting Principles Board (APB), resulting in the publication of Accounting Principles Board Opinion No. 5, *Reporting of Leases in Financial Statements of Lessee.* The opinion required that noncancelable leases be capitalized if they are deemed to be clearly in substance installment purchases of property. Needless to say, firms managed to write leasing contracts with covenants more compatible with noncapitalization. The Securities and Exchange Commission (SEC) and the APB intervened again in 1973 to require more detailed footnote disclosures in the APB Opinion No. 31, *Disclosure of Lease Commitments by Lessees* and Accounting Series Release (ASR) No. 147, *Notice of Adoption of Amendments to Regulation S-X Requiring Improved Disclosure of Leases* (1973). For example, ASR No. 147 called for (1) disclosure of a schedule of cash flow commitments for all noncancelable, noncapitalized leases whether financing operating (a) for each of the five years following the date of the last balance sheet, (b) for each of the following three five-year periods, and (c) for the term of the lease remaining after the next 20 years; and (2) disclosure of present values of noncancelable financing leases and average and range of discount rates used in computing those present values.

The SEC indicated at the same time that the FASB needed to address the issue, which led to the issuance in November 1976 of Statement No. 13 distinguishing between capital leases and operating leases (see Chapters 2 and 3).

MEASUREMENT OF THE CURRENT PORTION OF LONG-TERM OBLIGATION

The requirement of Statement No. 13 is to record the capital lease as an asset and an obligation with the stipulation that the obligations shall be separately identified in the balance sheet as obligations in classifying them with current and noncurrent liabilities in classified balance sheets. There is, however, no guideline for the measurement of the current portion of long-term obligations or receivables.[1] The two alternatives considered in most textbooks are the change in present value approach (CPV), and the present value of next year's payment approach (PVNYP). This results in different amounts being reflected as the current portion of a long-term obligation. The differences in the approaches can be described as follows.[2]

A. The CPV approach defines the current portion (CP) as

$$CP = L(1 + r)^{-n}$$

where

CP = current portions of long-term obligation
L = constant lease payment
r = interest rate
N = number of time periods until the last lease payment

B. The PVNYP approach defines the current portion as:

$$CP = L(1 + r)^{-1}$$

As an example let's assume a lease with \$10,000 lease payment where $n = 2$ and $r = 10$ percent. The current portion of long-term obligation is measured

A. Using the CPV approach as:
    $CP = \$20,000 \ (1.10)^{-2} = \$16,528.81$

B. Using the PVNYP as:
    $CP = \$20,000 \ (1.10)^{-1} = \$18,182.586$

The difference between the two amounts—\$1,653.776—does not seem material. However if n was equal to 20 years, then the current portion of long-term obligation using the CPV approach is:

$$CP = \$20,000 \ (1.10)^{-20} = \$2,972.818$$

The present value of next year's payment calculations is \$18,182.586. Given this awkward situation, Robert Sweringa recommends the following measure: "Given the potential significance of the current and non-current portion of lease obligations as well as other long-term receivables and payables in classifying balance sheets, perhaps the FASB should consider how these portions should be calculated and provide some guidelines."[3]

Given the problem raised by the existence of the two alternatives to the measurement of the current portion of long-term lease obligations, and the absence of FASB guidelines, there is obviously need for an investigation of actual practices on the matter. Accordingly, A. W. Richardson examined a sample of 170 companies randomly selected from a list of 1,461 companies on the New York Stock Exchange, showing that the change in present value approach appears to be dominant in current financial reporting practice.[4] In addition, the evidence showed that the adjustment of the reported financial statement numbers to those that would be obtained by the present value of next year's payments approach does not affect the ranking of companies by a number of financial measures. Accordingly, Richardson concludes:

> The results obtained for this randomly selected sample suggest that a uniform approach to determining the current portion of capital lease obligations exists in practice and that changing this approach would not have a significant effect on the ranking of companies in financial analysis. Consequently, it is not clear that the FASB should expend the resources to study this problem and issues guidelines as suggested by Sweringa (1984).[5]

CONSTRUCTIVE CAPITALIZATION

A lot of annual reports of large corporations are reporting very large noncancelable operating lease commitments. The deliberate choice of treating those leases as operating leases creates serious understatements of the asset and liability sides of their balance sheets and major distortions in key statement financial ratios. These operating leases are in fact de facto off-balance sheet investing/financing instruments with serious impacts on the risk and return measures used by users of financial accounting information in the evaluation of the financial soundness of these firms. The way to correct for the limitations associated with annual reports loaded with very large noncancelable operating lease commitments is to reconstruct their balance sheets as if the operating leases have been capitalized as financing leases, a method known as constructive capitalization.[6]

Constructive capitalization consist of changing the recording of leases as rented arrangements (operating leases) to asset purchases (capitalized leases) at their inception, and therefore showing the estimated unrecorded liability and assets. To illustrate the application of constructive capitalization, this section relies on the example used in E. A. Imhoff, R. C. Lipe, and D. W. Wright's study.[7] The example examined leasing instructions in the 1988 annual report of McDonald's Corporation, the world's largest chain of fast food restaurants. The relevant data are shown in Exhibit 4.1. The problem is to estimate the present value of the schedule minimum operating lease cash flows totaling about $2,236 million. Various assumptions are made:

Exhibit 4.1
McDonald's Corporation Financial Statement Data and Leasing Footnote

Panel A   ($ in 000,000)

Reported Total Assets	$8,159
Reported Total Liabilities	$4,746
Reported Total Stockholders' Equity	$3,413
Reported Net Income	$ 646
Reported Effective Book Tax Rate	38.3%

Panel B

At December 31, 1988, the Company was lessee at 1,636 restaurant locations under ground leases (the Company leases the land and constructs and owns the buildings) and at 1,922 locations under improved leases (lessor owns the land and buildings). These leases are operating leases except for the building portions of 485 leases, which together with certain restaurant equipment leases, are capital leases. Land and building lease terms are generally for 20 to 25 years and, in many cases, provide for rent escalations and one or more five-year renewal options with certain leases providing purchase options. The Company is generally obligated for the related occupancy costs which include property taxes, insurance and maintenance. In addition, the Company is lessee under noncancelable operating leases covering offices and vehicles.

At December 31, 1988, future minimum payments under capital leases and noncancelable operating leases, with initial terms of one year or more, are as follows:

		Operating leases		
(In thousands of dollars)	**Capital leases**	**Restaurant**	**Other**	**Total**
1989	$ 17,047	$ 152,834	$ 28,289	$ 181,123
1990	15,209	151,897	26,422	178,319
1991	13,926	147,962	20,199	168,161
1992	10,214	143,556	13,864	157,420
1993	6,983	138,142	10,234	148,376
Thereafter	52,504	1,336,377	65,980	1,402,357
Total	115,883	$2,070,768	$164,988	$2,235,756
Less imputed interest	50,196			
Present Value at December 31, 1988	$ 65,687			

Rent expense was as follows: 1988—$190 million; 1987—$160 million; and 1986—$143 million. Included in these amounts were percentage rents based on sales by the related restaurants in excess of minimum rents stipulated in certain capital and operating lease agreements as follows: 1988—$15 million; 1987—$12 million; and 1986—$11 million.

Source: Eugene A. Imhoff, Jr., Robert C. Lipe, and David W. Wright, "Operating Leases: Impact of Constructive Capitalization," *Accounting Horizons* (March 1991), p. 54. Reprinted with permission.

1. The examination of the debt footnote yielded a conservative measure for McDonald's historical interest rate averaging 10 percent.

2. The $1,402 million lump sum following 1993 is spread over 10 years resulting in an average cash flow per year beyond 1993 of $140.2 million per year ($1,402.357/10).

A capitalization of the cash flows using the annual 10 percent interest rate and 15-year average year remaining lease life is shown in Exhibit 4.2. It shows a present value of McDonald's unrecorded liability for operating lease commitments of about $1.17 billion. Changing the inter-

Exhibit 4.2
McDonald's Operating Leases: Equivalent Present Value ($ in millions)

Panel A: PV of Operating Leases

	Scheduled Cash Flows[a]	×	10% Present Value Factor	=	PV of Cash Flows
1989	181.1	×	.9091	=	$ 164.6
1990	178.3	×	.8264	=	147.3
1991	168.2	×	.7513	=	126.4
1992	157.4	×	.6830	=	107.5
1993	148.4	×	.6209	=	92.1
1994 to 2003	140.2[b]	×	3.8153[c]	=	534.9

$1,172.8 Estimated unrecorded debt

[a]Rounded to the nearest $100,000, and assuming all payments occur at the end of each year.
[b]$1,402.357/10 years = $140.2 per year
[c]This factor is the present value of a 15 year annuity at 10% less the present value of a 5 year annuity at 10%, based on assumed $140.2 million at the end of each year from 1994-2003.

Panel B: Sensitivity Analysis

Assumptions as above except—	Estimated Unrecorded Debt
1. If interest rate is 8 percent (not 10 percent)	$1,311.0 million
2. If interest rate is 12 percent (not 10 percent)	$1,057.3 million
3. If total remaining life is 20 years (not 15 years)	$1,079.4 million
4. If total remaining life is 25 years (not 15 years)	$1,008.6 million

Source: Eugene A. Imhoff, Jr., Robert C. Lipe, and David W. Wright, "Operating Leases: Impact of Constructive Capitalization," *Accounting Horizons* (March 1991), p. 55. Reprinted with permission.

est rate (+2 percent) and the remaining life of the lease (+5 or +10 years) provided a range of estimates going from a low of $1.01 billion to a high of $1.31 billion for the unrecorded debt attributable to the operating leases.

The next step is to estimate the unrecorded amount, which depends on the scheduled cash flows, incremental borrowing rate, remaining life of the lease, an estimate of the weighted average total life of the leased assets, and our assumed depreciation method. Exhibit 4.3 is used as a mechanism for estimating the unrecorded asset after estimating the unrecorded liability. The table's percentages express the unauthorized unrecorded operating lease asset as a percentage of the remaining unrecorded operating lease liability at various stages of the asset's weighted average remaining useful life.[8]

Using the assumed weighted average total life of 30 years with 15 years remaining, and the 10 percent interest rate, the implied net book value of the unrecorded asset is 62 percent of the estimated unrecorded liability. If the assumed weighted average life is changed to 25 years with 15 years remaining, the implied net book value is now 72 percent

Exhibit 4.3
Constructive Capitalization of Operating Leases: Relation Between Unrecorded Liability and Unrecorded Asset Over Time

Total Lease Life	Marginal Interest Rate	Ratio of Asset Balance to Liability Balance*							Point of Maximum Difference Between Asset and Liability
		% of Original Lease Life Expired							
		20%	30%	40%	50%	60%	70%	80%	
10	.08	93%	90%	87%	84%	81%	78%	75%	53%
15	.08	91	86	82	78	74	70	66	55%
20	.08	89	83	78	73	68	64	59	56%
25	.08	87	81	75	69	64	58	53	58%
30	.08	86	79	72	66	60	54	49	59%
10	.10	92	88	85	81	78	74	71	54%
15	.10	89	84	79	74	70	65	61	56%
20	.10	87	81	75	69	64	59	54	58%
25	.10	85	78	72	65	59	53	48	59%
30	.10	84	76	69	62	55	49	43	61%
10	.12	91	87	82	78	74	71	67	55%
15	.12	88	82	77	71	66	61	57	57%
20	.12	86	79	72	66	60	55	49	59%
25	.12	84	76	69	62	56	49	44	61%
30	.12	83	75	67	59	52	45	39	63%

*Ratio equals (RL/TL) times PV of annuity for TL at i%, divided by PV of annuity for RL at i%, where RL = remaining life, TL = total life and i% = marginal borrowing rate.

Source: Eugene A. Imhoff, Jr., Robert C. Lipe, and David W. Wright, "Operating Leases: Impact of Constructive Capitalization," *Accounting Horizons* (March 1991), p. 56. Reprinted with permission.

of the estimated unrecorded liability. The authors settled on the value of 67 percent yielding a value of $785.8 million for McDonald's leased assets if the operating leases have been capitalized. The total effects of this constructive capitalization scenario are shown in Exhibit 4.4, with a 9 percent decrease in ROA (rate of return in assets) and a 30 percent increase in D/E (debt/equity). The same constructive capitalization scenario is used on seven pairs of firms from seven industries.[9] The results reported in Exhibit 4.5 show that constructive capitalization of operating lease leads to a drastic and different financial picture, and may be essential for a sound financial analysis.

ECONOMIC CONSEQUENCES OF THE ADOPTION OF THE LEASE DISCLOSURE RULE

The previous example on constructive capitalization showed that the choice of capitalization increased the debt equity ratio by 30 percent from 1.35 times to 1.81 times. Therefore, firms may be motivated to move

Exhibit 4.4
**Impact of Constructive Capitalization of Operating Leases on
McDonald's Balance Sheet and Financial Ratios**

Panel A: Balance Sheet Impact

**Balance Sheet
December 31, 1988
($ in millions)**

Assets:	Liabilities:	
	Unrecorded Lease Liabilities	
	(See Table 2 Details)	$1,172.8[a]
Unrecorded Lease Assets	Tax Consequences (.4 × $387)	(154.8)[d]
(.67 × Liability) $785.8[b]	Net Liability Effect	$1,018.0
	Stockholders Equity:	
	Cumulative Effect on Retained	
	Earnings Net of Tax Consequences	
	($1,172.8 − $785.8 = $387) × (1 − .4)	(232.2)[e]
$785.8		$ 785.8

[a] Step 1—see Table 2 calculation
[b] Step 2—using Table 3
[c] Step 3—based on combined total marginal tax rate of 40 percent
[d] Step 4—either deferred income taxes or taxes payable depending on tax treatment of lease

Panel B: Impact on Financial Ratios

	Assets (ROA) Return on	Total Debt to Total Equity (D/E)
1) As reported based on annual report	$\frac{\$646}{\$8,159} = 7.9\%$	$\frac{\$4,746}{\$3,413} = 1.39$ times
2) As revised per panel A adjustments to balance sheet only	$\frac{\$646}{\$8,945} = 7.2\%$	$\frac{\$5,764}{\$3,181} = 1.81$ times
3) Percentage change $\left(\frac{(1-2)}{1}\right)$	9% Decrease in ROA	30% Increase in D/E

Source: Eugene A. Imhoff, Jr., Robert C. Lipe, and David W. Wright, "Operating Leases: Impact of Constructive Capitalization," *Accounting Horizons* (March 1991) p. 60. Reprinted with permission.

from capital leases to more operating leases as a way of reducing their leverage following the adoption of Financial Accounting Standard (FAS) No. 13. It is basically the hypothesis advanced and verified by Eugene Imhoff and Jacob Thomas that financial statement changes caused by FAS No. 13 increased the cost of using capital leases, thereby causing lessees to reduce the proportion of assets financed through capital leases.[10] They conclude as follows:

> Overall our results support the hypothesis that the financial statement effects of lease capitalization required by Statement of Financial Accounting Standard (SFAS) No. 13 had a significant impact on lessees. Capital leases as a source of financing declined sharply after the standard. The substantial amount of substitution into operating leases we observe suggests that renegotiation of lease con-

Exhibit 4.3

Impact of Constructive Capitalization of Operating Leases on Seven Industry Pairings

| Industry/ Company | As Reported ($ in millions) | | | Reported ROA | Revised ROA | % Change† | Reported D/E Multiple | Revised D/E Multipl3 | % Chang3† |
	Total Assets	Total Debt	Net Income*						
Home Furnishings									
Pier 1 Imports	$ 257.9	$ 163.8	$ 16.1	6.2%	4.0%	−55%	1.7	6.0	+243%
Rhodes, Inc.	261.5	152.0	11.9	4.6	4.1	−9	1.4	1.8	+30
Food Stores									
Winn-Dixie	1,417.7	678.3	112.3	7.9	5.3	−33	.9	2.8	+204
A&P (Great Atl. & Pac.)	2,248.2	1,391.9	103.4	4.6	4.0	−14	1.6	2.5	+50
Fast Food									
Foodmaker (Jack-in-box)	470.5	352.9	13.9	2.9	2.4	−19	3.0	5.6	+85
Church's Fried Chicken	344.8	86.3	9.5	2.8	2.6	−4	.3	.4	+25
Semi-Fast Food									
TGI Friday's	178.6	70.6	7.9	4.4	2.7	−38	.7	2.6	+302
Luby's Cafeteria	162.2	36.6	23.7	14.6	13.4	−8	.3	.4	+54
Clothing									
The Limited	1,587.9	858.8	235.2	14.8	9.6	−35	1.2	3.8	+222
Petrie Stores	1,134.3	595.8	47.5	4.2	3.5	−16	1.1	1.8	+64
Drug/Food Stores									
Walgreen Co.	1,362.0	739.6	103.5	7.6	5.6	−27	1.2	2.8	+134
American Stores	3,650.2	2,764.5	154.3	4.2	3.9	−9	3.1	4.0	+29
Airlines									
Delta	5,342.4	3,404.5	263.7	4.9	3.5	−29	1.8	4.4	+150
TWA	4,224.2	3,931.7	45.3	1.1	1.0	−9	13.5	23.8	+77
Average Percentage Changes									
High Lessee						−34%			+191%
Low Lessee						−10%			+47%

*Excluding Extraordinary Gains/Losses

†Based on non-rounded ratio values: (Actual-Revised)/Actual.

Source: Eugene A. Imhoff, Jr., Robert C. Lipe, and David W. Wright, "Operating Leases: Impact of Constructive Capitalization," *Accounting Horizons* (March 1991), p. 61. Reprinted by permission.

tracts is a low-cost alternative, relative to other responses that potentially mitigate the financial statement effects of the standard. To a lesser extent, other capital structure changes were also selected in some instances, evidenced by an increased use of nonlease financing (decreases in debt and increases in equity). Overall, most lessees apparently elected not to renegotiate contracts affected by lease capitalization nor to enter into technical default, and employed various capital structure changes instead.[11]

Given the above economic consequences in terms of the impact of the adoption of the disclosure rule mandated by SFAS No. 13 on the leverage portion of firms, the obvious research question is to determine the factors that affected managements' choices in accounting for leases prior to the implementation of SFAS No. 13. The research question, which fits well within the positive accounting paradigm, was examined by Samir El-Gazzar, Steve Lilien, and Victor Pastena.[12]

The three explanations for nonsectional differences in the choices for accounting for leases were: debt covenant constraint, compensation plans based on income, and political costs. Basically, a positive correlation between D/E and the operating method, between the increase in D/E and the operating method, between industry-adjusted D/E and the operating method, between the operating method and income-based compensation plans, and a negative correlation between sales and the operating method and between the effective tax rate and the operating method are expected. The results were generally in support of the positive impact of financial contracting and management bonus incentive variables. The political cost hypothesis was not supported while tax return considerations seem to influence management's lease accounting choice. The results from a positive accounting study point to the potential managerial concern for the balance sheet effect of lease capitalization. In fact, Mie Nakayma, Steve Lilien, and Martin Benis report that over 75 percent of the 176 companies opposing SFAS No. 13 explained their position by citing covenant violations or distortions of their debt-to-equity position.[13] This may explain why more firms renegotiated existing leases and modified the terms of new leases to avoid the capitalization required by SFAS No. 13.[14]

While most of the above studies focused on balance sheet effects, income effects seem to also argue for the adoption of the operating method. The point was illustrated by Ernst & Ernst[15] showing that reported income under the operating method is higher early in the life of a lease, because the rental expense under the operating method is less than the sum of the initial interest and depreciation expenses under cap-italization. While this advantage disappears at the end of the lease life, it continues if leasing activities continue to grow on a nominal basis. A complete examination of the economic consequences of the adoption of the disclosure rule prior to and following Statement No. 13 is provided by the following studies.

The effects of the lease capitalization in share prices by R. Bowman,[16] showed that prices behave as if financial leases are similiar to other forms of debt. A number conclusion was reached by J. E. Finnerty, R. N. Fitz-simmons, and T. W. Oliver[17] showing that share prices are not affected by prescription of capitalization, even though some prior work by B. T. Ro[18] implied that the release of information had an adverse effect on security pricing. Other examinations of the economic consequences of the adoption of the disclosure rule prior to and following Statement No. 13 are provided by A. R. Abdel-Khalik, R. B. Thompson, and T. W. Oliver[19] and by Abdel-Khalik.[20]

The first study focused on the impact of adoption ASR No. 147 *Notice of Adoption of Amendments to Regulation S-X Requiring Improved Disclosure of Leases*[21] and APB Opinion No. 31, *Disclosure of Lease Commitments by Lessees*[22] on the lessee's bond risk premium, and on the differences between the bond risk premiums of firms which utilize off-balance sheet lease financing and those of other firms that primarily finance through increase of capitalized long-term debt. The study is ba-sically an evaluation of the impact of footnote disclosure of debt on the bond risk premium as a measure of the debt market's assessment of default risk. The results show that the disclosure of present values of noncapitalized leases does not appear to significantly influence bond risk premiums of firms affected by the disclosure ruling, and the mean bond risk premiums of some firms that finance through noncapitalized financ-ing leases were significantly lower than mean bond risk premiums of the firms of similar risk profile. Abdel-Khalik et al. concluded as follows:

Taking these two findings together and assuming that (a) our sam-ples are representative and (b) the bond risk premium is an appro-priate measure of default risk, then it is arguable that some firms with material noncapitalized financing leases have enjoyed a rela-tively lower assessment of their default risk and that present value footnote disclosure has not altered this position. If our samples are not representative, then the same implications still apply but only to firms included in these samples. In either case, one may only speculate on what the impact of FASB Statement No. 13 might be on these types of firms. Since implementing Statement No. 13 will have the effect of moving the present values of these previously noncapitalized leases to long-term debt on the balance sheet, it is likely that we will observe a reassessment of default risk for these firms only if the implications drawn in this study are reasonably correct.[23]

The second study by Abdel-Khalik as the principal researcher focuses on the economic effects of lessees of FASB Statement No. 13.[24] Nine research questions were examined:

1. Does capitalization of leases have a major effect on the relationships of data within financial statements? The results showed, as expected, a decline in reported current ratio, an increase in debt/equity ratio, and a slight decrease in the accounting return on assets, especially for smaller companies with relatively significant leases than for larger companies with relatively significant leases.

2. What are the kinds of decisions that appear to have been made at the company level following lease capitalization? The actions that may be caused by the capitalization of exisisting lease contracts may include:

(a) early retirement of debt, (b) conversion of bonds to equity shares, (c) financing acquisitions by issuing equity shares, (d) making discretionary accounting changes, (e) increasing investment outlays as measured by capital expenditures, (f) renegotiating terms of existing lease contracts so they would not satisfy the criteria for capital leases, or (g) creating unconsolidated finance subsidiaries to which lease contracts would be assigned.[25]

The results showed that efforts have been made to structure the terms of new lease contracts or that capitalization could be avoided and that firms increased buying or constructing assets instead of leasing them. In addition, during a three-year period following the issuance of Statement No. 13 (1976–1978), the following unusual changes were examined: (a) increased retirements of long-term debt, (b) increased sales of equity shares, (c) decrease in outstanding convertible bonds, (d) decrease in the balance of treasury stock, (e) increased capital expenditures, (f) changes in the special items charged to income, and (g) increased acquisitions effected by issuing stocks. The observed unusual changes were in fact

(a) sale of common stock and preferred stock, (b) retirement of long-term debt, and (c) conversions of bonds to stock.

3. Have preparers of financial statements of lessee companies been motivated by the accounting change required by Statement No. 13 to alter their economic decisions given the cosmetic nature of the change? Some of the reasons why management may do so include (a) dividing covenant violations, (b) beliefs and perceptions held by preparers of financial statements about the reaction of others, and (c) management's incentive compensation.

4. Do the capitalization of leases influence analysts' evaluations? The results showed that the analysts indicated no adverse effects on the evaluation of lessees supporting a concern of some preparers of financial statements that the evaluation of success indicators by users may be influenced by cosmetic accounting changes.[26]

5. What are the effects of capitalization of leases on the markets' assessment of risk and return on the securities of firms? This is done by examining (a) market-based systematic risk of common stock, (b) bond ratings as a surrogate for systematic risk of common stock, (c) market-based unsystematic risk of common stock, (d) total variance of returns on common stock as a measure of total risk, (e) bond-risk premiums, (f) mean unexpected holiday returns on common stock, and (g) mean unexpected holiday returns on common bonds. The results indicate no significant association between the events leading up to the adoption of Statement No. 13 and the market-based measures.

6. How do users, preparers, and auditors of financial statements feel about the consistency between capitalization and the board objectives of financial statements? The responses disagreed with the ability to predict cash flow and the assessment of dividend-paying ability, and agreed with assessment of debt-paying ability.

7. What are the explicit negative views presented about the changes in lease disclosure requirements. The negative views focused on (a) the technical complexity and details of the standards, amendments, and interpretations of accounting for leases; (b) the arbitrary approach to determining the interest rate to be used in capitalization; (c) the administrative cost involved in compliance with the statement; (d) the negative effect on comparability of financial statements due to variation among companies in applying the rules; (e) the belief that the FASB has not demonstrated that disclosure under ASR 147 is inadequate compared with the alternative of capitalization; and (f) the elimination from disclosure of some data considered essential by financial analysts.[27]

8. How do users, preparers, and auditors of financial statements view certain possible changes in accounting for leases. The respondents were particularly in favor of (a) required footnote disclosure of a complete schedule of future cash flow commitments for all leases, and (b) continued measurement of annual expense charges as the amortization of the asset plus the interest on the debt.[28]

9. What are the lessons the researchers learned that could be of benefit to readers? The results indicate that (a) some of the actions that managers took were the result of conflict between the requirements of accounting standards and internal operating systems of their firms; (b) specifying a very tight set of criteria may lead to manipulation; (c) the perceptions, beliefs, and incentives of preparers play a major role in their actions to accounting standards; (d) a withdrawal of data used by users leads to unfavorable reactions about the accounting standards; (e) accounting standards and methods seem to have outpaced many users' knowledge, creating a gap and a lot of frustration; and (f) auditors have huge expectations of the favorable impact of the concepted framework on the standard-setting process.[29]

PREDICTIVE ABILITY OF FINANCIAL RATIOS BASED ON THE LEASE DISCLOSURES RATE

Because the capitalization method advocated by SFAS No. 13 led to a better representation of both the liability and asset position of a firm, it should be expected that the financial ratios based on capitalization were a better predictive ability of economic events than the financial ratios based on the operating method. In fact, most of the predictive ability studies that followed the adoption of SFAS No. 13 managed to compute the leverage ratio but included the additional liability created by capitalization of the financial lease payments.[30] It is, however, appropriate to note that the one predictive ability study preceding the adoption of SFAS No. 13 did not support the hypothesis that addition of capitalized lease data to a firm's financial statements will increase the power of affected financial ratios for predicting firm bankruptcy.[31] Those results are not representative of the situation following the adoption of SFAS No. 13. As noted in the conclusion of the study: "This conclusion does not necessarily mean that leases should not be capitalized because lease data may be important for other uses of the financial statements not examined in this research. Additional research, employing other criteria, can produce more information about the effect of capitalized leases."[32]

Although this study did not find differences in the power of financial ratios to predict bankruptcy when ratios are computed with or without capitalizing long-term leases, the Zeta model developed by E. I. Altman, R. G. Haldeman, and P. Narayanaw,[33] which includes a capitalization of all noncancelable operating and financial leases, resulted in a model that had better accuracy rates than the existing bankruptcy prediction models. Rick Elam's results are surprising since lease capitalization requirements do cause an apparent deterioration in firms' debt-equity ratios.[34,35] So, it is not surprising that Trevor Williams and Ian Zimmer,[36] in an experimental study evaluating the effects of alternative methods of accounting for leases, found that the reporting methods affected the behavior of financial analysts in projecting earnings but not in share valuations. Similarily, M. W. Dirsmith and J. B. Thies[37] relied on a survey of corporate executives to evaluate the impact of lessee accounting rules on management decisions. Their results show that (1) factors of economic substance have more of an impact on lease-purchase decision making than factors which primarily concern the form in which information is reported; and (2) reporting entities characterized as being financially weak consider form factors—that is, off-balance-sheet financing—to have a greater impact on lease-purchase decision making than do financially strong companies.[38]

CONCLUSION

This chapter examined some of the important issues associated with the adoption of Statement No. 13 in accounting for leases. The issues examined included (1) a history of the accounting rules, (2) the financial statements effects of the lease disclosure rule, (3) the measurement of the current portion of long-term lease obligation, (4) the constructive capitalization scenario, (5) the empirical studies in the economic consequences of the adoption of the disclosure rule, and (6) the predictive ability of financial ratios based on the lease disclosure rule.

NOTES

1. Harold E. Wyman, and Wesley T. Andrews, Jr., ''Classifying the Receivable in a Lease Transaction: A Dilemma,'' *The Accounting Review* (October 1975), pp. 905–908.

2. Robert J. Sweringa, ''When Current Is Noncurrent and Vice Versa,'' *The Accounting Review* (January 1984), pp. 123–130.

3. Ibid., p. 130.

4. A. W. Richardson, "The Measurement of the Current Portion of Long-Term Lease Obligations: Some Evidence from Practice," *The Accounting Review* (October 1985), pp. 744–752.

5. Ibid., p. 752.

6. E. A. Imhoff, Jr., R. C. Lipe, and D. W. Wright, "Operating Leases: Impact of Constructive Capitalization," *Accounting Horizons* (March 1991), pp. 51–63.

7. Ibid.

8. The following assumptions are made: (a) Straight line depreciation is the method used; (b) Both the unrecorded lease asset and the unrecorded lease liability are 100 percent of the percent value of future lease payments at the inception of each lease; (c) The unrecorded lease asset and the unrecorded lease liability are both zero after the lease payment is made for each lease.

9. The constructive capitalization relied on the following six uniform assumptions: (a) The interest rate for each firm is 10 percent; (b) The average remaining life of the operating leases is 15 years; (c) All the scheduled cash flows take place at year end; (d) The unrecorded asset is equal to 70 percent of the unrecorded debt; (e) The combined effective tax rate is 40 percent; (f) The effect on the current period's net income is zero.

10. Eugene A. Imhoff and Jacob K. Thomas, "Economic Consequences of Accounting Standards: The Lease Disclosure Rule Change," *Journal of Accounting and Economics* (December 1988), pp. 277–310.

11. Ibid., p. 305.

12. Samir El-Gazzar, Steve Lilien, and Victor Pastena, "Accounting for Leases by Lessees," *Journal of Accounting and Economics* (October 1986), pp. 217–238.

13. Mie Nakayma, Steven Lilien, and Martin Benis, "Due Process and FAS No. 13," *Management Accounting*, 27, (1981), pp. 49–53.

14. R. Abdel-Khalik, *Economic Effects on Lessees of FASB Statement No. 13: Accounting for Leases* (Stamford, CT: FASB, 1981).

15. Ernst & Ernst, *Accounting for Leases, Financial Reporting Developments*, Retrieval no. 38574 (New York: Ernst & Ernst, March 1977).

16. R. Bowman, "The Theoretical Relationship Between Systematic Risk and Financial (Accounting) Variables," *Journal of Finance* (June 1978).

17. J. E. Finnerty, R. N. Fitzsimmons, and T. W. Oliver, "Lease Capitalization and Systematic Risk," *The Accounting Review* (October 1978), pp. 631–649.

18. B. T. Ro, "The Disclosure of Capitalized Lease Information and Stock Prices," *Journal of Accounting Research* (Autumn 1978), pp. 315–340.

19. A. R. Abdel-Khalik, R. B. Thompson, and R. E. Taylor, "The Impact of Reporting Leases off the Balance Sheet on Bond Risk Premiums: Two Exploratory Studies," in *Economic Consequences of Financial Accounting Standards* (Stamford, CT: FASB, 1978), pp. 103–157.

20. Abdel-Khalik, *Economic Effects on Lessees.*

21. Securities and Exchange Commission, *Notice of Adoption of Amendments to Regulation S-X Requiring Improved Disclosure of Leases, Accounting Series Release No. 147* (October 1973).

22. American Institute of Certified Public Accountants, Accounting Principles Board, APB Opinion No. 31, *Disclosure of Leases Commitments by Lessees* (December 1973).

23. Abdel-Khalik, Thompson, and Taylor, "The Impact of Reporting Leases off the Balance Sheet," pp. 151–152.

24. Abdel-Khalik, *The Economic Effects on Lessees.*

25. Ibid., p. 18.

26. Ibid., p. 24.

27. Ibid., p. 25.

28. Ibid., p. 31.

29. Ibid., p. 32.

30. Ahmed Belkaoui, *Industrial Bond Ratings and the Rating Process* (Westport, CT: Greenwood Press, 1983).

31. Rick Elam, "The Effect of Lease Data on the Predictive Ability of Financial Ratios," *The Accounting Review* (January 1975), pp. 25–43.

32. Ibid., p. 41.

33. E. I. Altman, R. G. Haldeman, and P. Narayanaw, "Zeta Analysis: A New Model to Identify Bankruptcy Risk of Corporations," *Journal of Banking and Finance*, 1 (1977).

34. D. C. Chamberlain, "Capitalization of Lease Obligations," *Management Accounting* (December 1975); and Elam, "The Effect of Lease Data."

35. D. Palmon and M. Kwatinez, "The Significant Role Interpretation Plays in the Implementation of SFAS No. 13," *Journal of Accounting, Auditing and Finance* (Spring 1980).

36. Trevor Williams and Ian Zimmer, "The Effects of Alternative Methods of Accounting for Leases—An Experimental Study," *Abacus*, 15, 1 (1983), pp. 64–75.

37. M. W. Dirsmith and J. B. Thies, "The Impact of Lessee Accounting Rules on Management Decisions," *Review of Business and Economic Research*, 5 (1976), pp. 26–35.

38. Ibid., p. 34.

SELECTED READINGS

Abdel-Khalik, R. *Economic Effects on Lessees of FASB Statement No. 13: Accounting for Leases* (Stamford, CT: FASB, 1981).

Baker, C. R. "Leasing and Setting Accounting Standards: Mapping the Labyrinth." *Journal of Auditing Accounting and Finance* (Spring 1980).

Benjamin, J. J. "FASB Statement No. 13 in Retrospect and Prospect." *CPA Journal* (June 1977).

Elam, Erik. "The Effect of Lease Data on the Predictive Ability of Financial Ratios." *The Accounting Review* (January 1975), pp. 25–43.

El-Gazzar, Samir, Steve Lilien, and Victor Pastena. "Accounting for Leases by Lessees." *Journal of Accounting and Economics* (October 1986), pp. 221–238

Finnerty, J. E., R. N. Fitzsimmons, and T. W. Oliver. "Lease Capitalization and Systematic Risk." *The Accounting Review* (October 1978).

Gritta, R. D. 'The Impact of Capitalization of Leases on Financial Analysis." *Financial Analysts Journal* (March–April 1974).

Imhoff, E. A. Jr., R. C. Lipe, and D. W. Wright. "Operating Leases: Impact of Constructive Capitalization." *Accounting Horizons* (March 1991).

Imhoff, E. A. Jr. and Jacob K. Thomas. "Economic Consequences of Accounting Standards: The Lease Disclosure Rule Change." *Journal of Accounting and Economics* (December 1988), pp. 277–310.

Nakayma, Nie, Steve Lilian, and Martin Benis. "Due Process and FAS No. 13." *Management Accounting*, 27 (1981), pp. 49–53.

Nelson, A. T. "Capitalizing Leases—The Effect on Financial Ratios." *Journal of Accountancy*, (July 1963).

Richardson, A. W. "The Measurement of the Current Portion of Long-Term Lease Obligations: Some Evidence from Practice." *The Accounting Review* (October 1985).

Ro, B. T. "The Disclosure of Capitalized Lease Information and Stock Prices." *Journal of Accounting Research* (Autumn 1978).

Sweringa, Robert J. "When Current Is Noncurrent and Vice Versa." *The Accounting Review* (January 1984), pp. 123–130.

Williams, Trevor and Ian Zimmer. "The Effects of Alternative Methods of Accounting for Leases—An Experimental Study." *Abacus* (June 1983), pp. 64–75.

Wyman, Harold E. and Wesley T. Andrews, Jr. "Classifying the Receivable in a Lease Transaction: A Dilemma." *The Accounting Review* (October 1975), pp. 905–908.

5

The Economics of Buying

Rather than leasing, management may often decide to buy a new machine. They make many general, nonrecurring investment decisions involving fixed assets, or *capital budgeting* decisions. Capital budgeting involves a current outlay or a series of outlays of cash resources in return for anticipated benefits to be received beyond one year in the future. The capital budgeting decision has three distinguishing characteristics: anticipated benefits, a time element, and a degree of risk associated with the realization of the benefits. In general, these characteristics can be described more specifically as anticipated cash benefits, a time lag between the initial capital investment and the realization of the cash benefits, and a degree of risk. However, investments with potentially large benefits are generally possible only with high risk and may require more time than investments with lower benefits.

Given these less-than-ideal relationships between the dimensions of a capital budgeting decision, management should desire a trade-off between these elements in making a capital budgeting decision that will meet their objectives. Although various objective functions may be chosen by firms, the most useful for evaluating capital budgeting decisions is the stockholders' wealth maximization model (SWMM).[1] Despite the fact that it represents a normative model, the SWMM provides a generally acceptable and meaningful criterion for the evaluation of capital budgeting proposals: the maximization of owners' wealth.

ADMINISTRATION OF CAPITAL BUDGETING

Although the administrative process of capital budgeting may differ from one firm to another, it involves five basic steps. The first step is planning, or origination and specification, of capital investments. Because capital investments are considered essential to a firm's profitable long-run growth, managers constantly search for new methods, processes, plants, and products. These projects usually come from various sources, including (1) new products or markets, and the expansion of existing products or markets; (2) research and development; (3) replacement of fixed assets; and (4) other investments to reduce costs, improve the quality of the product, improve morale, or comply with government orders, labor agreements, insurance policy terms, and so forth.

The second step in capital budgeting is the evaluation of the proposed capital investments. Firms differ in their routine for processing capital budgets, but most evaluate and approve the projects at various managerial levels. For example, a request for capital investment made by the production department may be examined, evaluated, and approved by (1) the plant managers, (2) the vice-president for operations, and (3) a capital budget committee or department, which may submit recommendations to the president. The president, after adding recommendations, may submit the project to the board of directors. This routine is often complemented and simplified by a uniform policy and procedure manual presenting in detail the firm's capital budgeting philosophy and techniques.

The third step in capital budgeting is the decision making based on the results of the evaluation process. Depending on the size of the projects, some decisions may be made at a high level, such as the board of directors (if they are large projects), or at a lower level if they are small- to medium-sized projects.

The fourth step is control. The firm includes each of the accepted projects in the capital budget and appropriates funds. Periodically, control is exercised over the expenditures made for the project. If the appropriated funds are made insufficient, a budgetary review can be initiated to examine and approve the estimated overrun. The control step can be extended to include a continuous evaluation process to incorporate current information and check the validity of the original predictions.

The fifth capital budgeting step is the postaudit. This involves a comparison of the actual cash flows of a capital investment with those planned and included in the capital budget.

ESTIMATING CASH FLOWS

One of the most important capital budgeting tasks for the evaluation of the project's capital investments is the estimation of the *relevant cash flows* for each project, which refers to the incremental cash flow arising from each project. Because companies rely on accrual accounting rather than cash accounting, adjustments are necessary to derive the cash flows from the conventional financial accounting records.

Cash and Accrual Accounting

Capital budgeting determines a project's potential incremental cash inflows and outflows compared with the flows if the project were not initiated. The receipt and payment of cash is the significant event in recording the cash inflows and outflows and determining the cash income of a project. This cash income, however, differs in the following ways from the accounting income due to the timing differences arising from the use of accrual accounting for external reporting:

1. The first difference arises from the capitalization of the cost of a capital asset at the time of purchase and the recognition of depreciation expenses over the asset's economic life. In a capital budgeting context, the cost of a capital asset is a cash outflow when paid.

2. Accrual accounting rests on the application of the matching of revenues and expenses, which leads to the recognition of revenues when earned and costs when incurred, even if no cash has been received or paid. This leads to the recognition of accounts receivable, accounts payable, and various asset balances as the result of the timing differences between accounting income and cash income.

To determine the cash income, adjustments in the accounting income are necessary to correct for these timing differences. Some adjustments are illustrated in Exhibit 5.1.

Exhibit 5.1
Reconciliation of Cash Flow and Accounting Income

1. Accounting Income (Traditional income Statement)

Assume that the purchase of a new machine costing $10,000 and having a ten-year and zero disposal value is expected

to earn the following for the first year:

Sales	$10,000
Less: Operating Expenses, Excluding Depreciation	$ 5.000
Depreciation (Straight-line)	1,000
Total expenses	$ 6,000
Operating Income before Income Taxes	$ 4.000
Less: Income Taxes at 40 Percent	1,600
Net Income after Taxes	$ 2,400

Other Accrual Information:
a. Sales are 40 percent cash.
b. The expenses, excluding depreciation, are 60 percent on credit.

2. Cash Flow (Cash Effects of Operations)

a. *Cash Inflow from Operation*	
Total Sales	$10,000
Less: Credit Sales: 60 Percent of $10,000 (Increase in Accounts Receivable)	6,000
Cash Collections from Sales	$ 4,000
b. *Cash Outflow from Operating Expenses*	
Total Expenses	$ 5,000
Less: Credit Expenditures: 60 Percent of $5,000 (Increase in Accounts Payable)	$ 3,000
Cash Payments for Operating Expenses	$ 2.000
c. *Net Cash Inflow:* $4,000 - $2,000	$ 2,000
d. *Income Tax Outflow*	$ 1,600
e. *After-Tax Net Cash Inflow*	$ 400
f. *Effect of Depreciation*	
Depreciation	$ 1,000
Tax at 50%	500
Tax Shield	$ 500
g. *Total Cash Flow* (After-Tax Net Cash Inflow + Tax Shield)	$ 900

Identifying the Project Cash Flows

Project cash flows are incremental cash flows arising from a project and are equal to the difference between the cash inflows and the cash outflows. The cash inflows include (1) after-tax net cash revenues, (2) savings in operating expenses, and (3) the salvage value of equipment from each project. The cash outflows include the cost of investment in each of the projects.

Effect of Charges on Cash Flows

Various charges affect the computation of cash flows. *Depreciation* and *amortization charges* are noncash expenses. However, they have an indirect influence on cash flow. Because depreciation is cash deductible, it provides a tax shield by protecting from taxation an amount of income equal to the depreciation deduction. The after-tax proceeds of a project are increased by the allowable depreciation times the tax rate, as shown by the following relationships:

$$\begin{matrix} \text{After-tax} \\ \text{cash} \\ \text{proceeds} \end{matrix} = \text{Revenues} - \begin{matrix} \text{Expenses} \\ \text{other than} \\ \text{depreciation} \end{matrix} - \text{Income tax} \qquad [1]$$

The income tax can be determined as follows:

$$\text{Income tax} = \text{Tax rate} \times \text{Taxable income} \qquad [2]$$

or

$$\text{Income tax} = \text{Tax rate} \times (\text{Revenues} - \begin{matrix} \text{Expenses} \\ \text{other than} \\ \text{depreciation} \end{matrix} - \text{Depreciation}). \qquad [3]$$

Therefore, the higher the depreciation, the lower the income tax.

By substituting equation 3 into equation 1, the after-tax proceeds can be expressed as follows:

$$\begin{matrix} \text{After-tax} \\ \text{cash} \\ \text{proceeds} \end{matrix} = \left[(1 - \text{Tax rate}) (\text{Revenues} - \begin{matrix} \text{Expenses} \\ \text{other than} \\ \text{depreciation} \end{matrix} \right] + (\text{Tax rate} \times \text{Depreciation}).$$

Financing charges are excluded from the cash flow computation used in capital budgeting. First, the interest factor would be counted twice by the use of present value methods of evaluation (to be presented in the next section). Second, the evaluation of a capital project is separate from and independent of the financing aspects.

Opportunity costs of scarce resources diverted from other uses because of the capital project should be charged against the investment project. They can be measured by estimating how much the resource (personnel time or facility space) would earn if the investment project were not undertaken.

RANKING CAPITAL PROJECTS

The project evaluation phase consists of evaluating the attractiveness of the investment proposals. Managers first choose the project evaluation methods best suited to the capital budgeting decision. The most common are the *discounted cash flow (DCF) methods, internal rate of return (IRR) method, net present value (NPV) method, profitability index (PI), payback method,* and *accounting rate of return (ARR) method.* Each of these methods will be examined in the following sections.

DISCOUNTED CASH FLOW METHODS

The discounted cash flow methods consider the *time value of money* in the evaluation of capital budgeting proposals. A dollar received now is worth more than a dollar received in the future; a dollar in the hand today can be invested to earn a return. Hence, to understand the DCF methods, it is necessary to grasp the time value concepts.

The DCF methods focus on cash flows generated over the life of a project rather than the accounting income. These methods involve discounting the cash flow of a project to its *present value* using an appropriate discount rate. There are two basic DCF methods: (1) the internal rate of return (or time-adjusted rate of return) method, and (2) the net present value method.

Internal Rate of Return Method

The IRR is the interest rate that equates the present value of an investment's cash flows and the cost of the investment. The IRR equation follows:

$$\sum_{t=0}^{n} \left[\frac{C_t}{(1 + r)^t} \right] = 0,$$

where

C_t = Cash flow for a period t, whether it be a net inflow or a net outflow, including the initial investment at $t = 0$.

n = Investment life—that is, the last period in which a cash flow is expected.

r = IRR as the discount rate that equates the present value of cash flow C_t to zero.

If the initial cash outlay or cost occurs at a time 0, the IRR equation becomes

$$\sum_{t=1}^{n}\left[\frac{C_t}{(1+r)^t}\right] - C_0 = 0.$$

Solving for r is on a trial-and-error basis; the procedures differ depending on whether the cash flows are uniform or nonuniform.

Uniform Cash Flows

To illustrate, assume a project considered by the Camelli Corporation requires a cash outlay of $39,100 and has an expected after-tax annual net cash savings of $10,000 for six years and no salvage value. Find the interest rate (r) that equates the present value of future annual cash flows of $10,000 and the initial outlay of $39,100 at time 0. Experimenting with two discount rates, 12 and 14 percent, you find

Discount Rate	Discount Factor	Cash Flow	Present Value of Stream
12%	4.1110	$10,000	$41,110
14%	3.8890	$10,000	$38,890

Thus, the IRR that equates the present value of the stream of annual savings and $39,100 is between 12 and 14 percent. This rate can be found by interpolating between 12 and 14 percent:

```
12% $41,110 (Too large)
14      38,890 (Too small)
 2% $ 2,220
```

$$\frac{\$41,110 - \$39,100}{\$2,220} = 0.905.$$

IRR $= 12\% + (0.905 \times 2\%) = 13.81\%.$

Exhibit 5.2
Amortization Schedule: Proof for the Internal Rate of Return

Year	Unrecorded Investment at Beginning of Year	Annual Cash Savings	13.81 % Return or Interest[a]	Cost Recovery[b]	Unrecorded Investment at End of Year[c]
1	$39,100.00	$10,000	$5399.71	$4600.29	$34,499.71
2	34,499.71	10,000	4764.41	5235.59	29,264.12
3	29,264.12	10,000	4041.38	5958.62	23,305.50
4	23,305.50	10,000	3218.49	6781.51	16,523.99
5	16,523.99	10,000	2281.96	7718.04	8,805.95
6	8,805.95	10,000	1216.10	8783.90	22.05[d]

[a]Return = Unrecorded investment × 13.81%.

[b]Cost recovery = Annual cash savings - Return.

[c]Cnrecorded investment at the end of the year = Unrecorded investment at the beginning of the

year - Cost recovery.

[d]Rounding error.

A trial-and-error process determines that 13.81 percent is the IRR that equates the present value of the stream of savings and the cost of investment. This indicates that the investment will yield a return of 13.81 percent per year in addition to recovering the original cost of $39,100. Exhibit 5.2 depicts the amortization schedule of the investment: The six-year cash savings of $10,000 recovers the original investment plus an annual return of 13.81 percent on the investment.

The computation of the IRR does not determine if the project is to be accepted or rejected. To do so, the IRR generally is compared with a required rate of return. The required rate of return, also known as the *cut-off rate* or *hurdle rate*, is the firm's cost of capital (the cost of acquiring funds). Passing the test does not mean the project will be funded, as funds may be required.

Nonuniform Cash Flows

The following example illustrates a project yielding cash flows that are not equal for all of the periods of the project's life. We assume the machine considered by the Camelli Corporation costs $39,100 and yields the following cash savings:

Year	Cash Savings
1	$20,000
2	14,000
3	10,000
4	6,000
5	5,000
6	4,000

Solving for the IRR that equates the present value of these savings and the cost of the investment also requires trial and error. First, experimenting with an interest rate of 16 percent, we find

Year	Discount Factor	× Cash Savings	= Present Value of Cash Savings
1	0.862	$20,000	$17,240
2	0.743	14,000	10,402
3	0.641	10,000	6,410
4	0.552	6,000	3,312
5	0.476	5,000	2,380
6	0.410	4,000	1,640

Present Value of Cash Savings	$41,384
Present Value of Cash Outflow	
(Cost of the Machine)	39,100
Difference	$ 2,284

Given the present value of cash savings is $2,284 higher than the present value of the cash outflow, the IRR must be higher than 16 percent.

Second, experimenting with an interest rate of 20 percent, we find

Year	Discount Factor	× Cash Savings	= Present Value of Cash Savings
1	0.833	$20,000	$16,660
2	0.694	14,000	9,716
3	0.579	10,000	5,790
4	0.482	6,000	2,892
5	0.402	5,000	2,010
6	0.335	4,000	1,340

Present Value of Cash Savings		$38,408
Present Value of Cash Outflow		
(Cost of Machine)		39,100
Difference (NPV)		$ (692)

Given the present value of cash savings is $692 lower than the present value of the cash outflow, the IRR must be *between* 16 and 20 percent. Third, experimenting with 19 percent we obtain

Year	Discount Factor	× Cash Savings	= Present Value of Cash Savings
1	0.840	$20,000	$16,800
2	0.706	14,000	9,884
3	0.593	10,000	5,930
4	0.499	6,000	2,994
5	0.419	5,000	2,095
6	0.352	4,000	1,408
Present Value of Cash Savings			$39,111
Present Value of Cash Outflow			
(Cost of the Machine)			39,100
Difference (NPV)			$ 11

Given that the present value of cash savings is only $11 higher than the cost of the machine, the IRR is approximately 19 percent.

Net Present Value Method

The NPV method compares the cost of an investment with the present value of the future cash flows of the investment at a selected rate of return, or hurdle rate. The NPV of an investment is

$$NPV = \sum_{t=1}^{n} \left[\frac{C_t}{(1 + r)^t} \right] - C_0,$$

where

C_t = Project cash flows.

r = Selected hurdle rate.

n = Project life.

C_0 = Cost of the investment.

If the NPV is greater than or equal to zero, the project is deemed acceptable, but it may not be funded if there is rationing. The required rate of return, or hurdle rate, is usually the cost of capital. The NPV procedure differs depending upon whether the cash flows are uniform or non-uniform.

Uniform Cash Flows

To illustrate the NPV method, let us return to the Camelli Corporation example in which a new machine costing $39,100 would yield an annual cash savings of $10,000 for the six years of its life. Assuming a cost of capital of 10 percent, the NPV of the project can be stated as follows:

$$NPV = \sum_{t=1}^{6} \left[\frac{\$10,000}{(1 + 0.10)^6} \right] - \$39,100.$$

The discount rate chart shows the present value of a constant stream of $1 received at the end of each year for N years at r percent. The appropriate discount factor for the Camelli Corporation is 4.355. Thus, the NPV is computed as follows:

$$NPV = (\$10,000 \times 4.355) - \$39,100 = \$4,450.$$

Given that the NPV is greater than zero, the Camelli Corporation should accept the new machine proposal. The positive NPV indicates that the Camelli Corporation will earn a higher rate of return on its investment than its cost of capital.

Different NPV's result from different hurdle rates. For example,

$$NPV \text{ at an } 8\% \text{ required rate} = (\$10,000 \times 4.623) - \$39,100 = \$7,130.$$
$$NPV \text{ at a } 14\% \text{ required rate} = (\$10,000 \times 3.889) - \$39,100 = \$(210).$$

Thus, given a stream of uniform cash flows, the higher the hurdle rate, the less attractive any investment proposal becomes.

The NPV method rests on two assumptions: (1) the cash flows are *certain* (this applies also to the IRR), and (2) the original investment can be viewed as either borrowed or loaned by the Camelli Corporation at the hurdle rate. Thus, if the Camelli Corporation borrows $39,100 from

Exhibit 5.3
Amortization Schedule Underlying the Net Present Value

Option 1 : Borrow and Invest in the Project

Year	Loan Balance at Beginning of Year	Interest at 10% per Year	Loan and Interest at End of Year	Cash Flow to Repay the Loan	Loan Balance at End of Year
1	$39,100.00	$3,910.00	$43,010.00	$10,000	$33,010.00
2	33,010.00	3,301.00	36,311.00	10,000	26,311.00
3	26,311.00	2,631.10	28,942.10	10,000	18,942.10
4	18,942.10	1,894.21	20,836.31	10,000	10,836.31
5	10,836.31	1,083.63	11,919.94	10,000	1,919.94
6	1,919.94	191.99	2,111.93	10,000	(7,888.06)

Option 2: Invest $4,450 at 10 Percent Rate of Return

Year	Investment Balance at Beginning of Year	Interest at 10% per Year	Investment and Interest at End of Year
1	$4,450.00	$445.00	$4,895.00
2	4,895.00	489.50	5,385.50
3	5,384.50	538.45	5,922.95
4	5,922.95	592.30	6,515.95
5	6,515.25	651.53	7,166.78
6	7,166.78	716.88	7,833.46[a]

[a]The $4.60 difference between $7,888.06 and $7,883.46 is a rounding error.

Note:

The above result for option 2 could be computed by simply multiplying $4,450 by the appropriate compound sum factor.

the bank at 10 percent and uses the cash flows generated to repay the loan, it will obtain the same return as if it had invested $4,450 at the same rate. (See Exhibit 5.3)

Nonuniform Cash Flows

The following example illustrates a project yielding cash flows that are not equal for all periods of the project's life. Assume again that the machine considered by the Camelli Corporation yields annual cash savings of $20,000, $14,000, $10,000, $6,000, $5,000, and $4,000 for the six years, respectively, and the cost of capital is 10 percent. The computation of the NPV follows:

Year	Discount Factor	× Cash Savings	= Present Value of Cash Savings
1	0.909	$20,000	$18,180
2	0.826	14,000	11,546
3	0.753	10,000	7,530
4	0.683	6,000	4,098
5	0.621	5,000	3,105
6	0.564	4,000	2,256
Present Value of Cash Savings			$46,733
Present Value of Cash Outflow			
(Cost of the Machine)			39,100
Difference (NPV)			$ 7,633

The NPV method is easier to apply than the IRR method with nonuniform cash flows, because it does not require iterative numerical methods.

Profitability Index

The PI, or benefit cost ratio, is another form of the NPV method. It is generally expressed as

$$PI = \frac{\text{Present value of cash inflows}}{\text{Present value of cash outflows}}.$$

For the Camelli Corporation example with uniform cash flows, the PI would be

$$PI = \frac{\$43,550}{\$39,100} = 1.114$$

For the Camelli Corporation example with nonuniform cash flows, the PI would be

$$PI = \frac{\$46,733}{\$39,100} = 1.195$$

The decision rule when evaluating different projects is to choose the project with the highest PI.

The NPV and the PI result in the same acceptance or rejection decision for any given project. However, the NPV and the PI can give different rankings for the mutually exclusive projects. In such a case, the NPV method is the preferred method; it expresses the absolute profitability of a project, whereas the PI expresses the relative profitability.

Comparison Between Net Present Value and Internal Rate of Return

Acceptance or Rejection Decision

The IRR and NPV methods lead to the same acceptance or rejection decisions for independent projects with one or more periods of outlays followed *only* by periods of net cash inflows. Exhibit 5.4 illustrates both the NPV and IRR applied to a capital project. At the zero discount rate, the NPV is equal to the sum of the total cash inflows less the total cash outflows. As the discount rate increases, the NPV decreases. Where the NPV reaches zero, the discount rate corresponds to the IRR, which is 20 percent in the fictional example depicted in Exhibit 5.4. The following situations are possible:

1. If the required rate of return used as a discount rate is less than the IRR, the project is acceptable under both methods. For example, if the required rate of return is 15 percent, the project is acceptable under both methods, given that at that rate Exhibit 5.4 shows an NPV superior to zero and a required rate of return inferior to the 20 percent IRR.

2. If the required rate of return is equal to the IRR, the project is acceptable under both methods. In such a case the NPV is equal to zero, and the required rate of return is equal to the IRR.

3. If the required rate of return is higher than the IRR, the project is not acceptable under either method.

Conflicts Between Net Present Value and Internal Rate of Return

The NPV and the IRR methods may lead to conflicting rankings. Which method provides the best result? To answer this question, the

Exhibit 5.4
Relationship Between Net Present Value and Internal Rate of Return

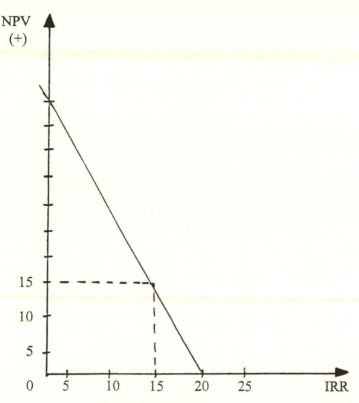

main conflicts between NPV and IRR must be examined, along with the problems associated with each of the methods.

The conflicts arise mainly in comparing mutually exclusive projects (projects capable of performing the same function). The evaluation of mutually exclusive projects by the NPV and the IRR methods can lead to at least three problems:

1. The problem when the mutually exclusive projects have different initial outlays is called the *scale effects problem.*

2. The problem when the mutually exclusive projects have a different timing of cash flows is called the *timing effects problem.*

3. The problem when the mutually exclusive projects have different lives is called the *live effects problem.*

Exhibit 5.5
Mutually Exclusive Investments: Scale Effects

Project	Initial Outlay	Cash Inflow (End of Year 1)	NPV at 15%	IRR
X	$ 8,333	$10,000	$362.7	20%
Y	$16,949	$20,000	$442.4	18%
W	$ 8,616	$10,000	$ 79.7	15.10%

Other problems arise from possible *multiple rates of return* when using the IRR method. Both the conflicts and problems identified will be examined before we judge which method provides the best ranking.

Scale Effects. The NPV and the IRR methods yield conflicting rankings when mutually exclusive projects having different initial outlays are compared. Consider the example in Exhibit 5.5, where project X is ranked better with the IRR method, and project Y is ranked better with the NPV method.

Given this conflicting result, which project should be chosen? Projects X and Y are incorrectly ranked by the IRR method because of the large difference in the cost of the projects. The incremental cost of $8,616 for project Y can be seen as an additional project W, which yields a positive NPV of $79.70 and an IRR of 15.10 percent, which is greater than the required rate of return of 15 percent. The incremental cost is acceptable under both the IRR and the NPV methods; thus, project Y should be selected. Since the NPV method has selected project Y, the NPV method is preferable.

Timing Effects. The NPV and IRR methods also yield conflicting results when mutually exclusive projects of equal size but with different timing of cash flows are compared. Consider the example in Exhibit 5.6, where project Y is ranked better with the IRR method, and project X is ranked better with the NPV method.

Given this conflicting result, should project X or Y be chosen? Again, use the incremental approach:

Year 0: $0 cash outlays for both projects.

Year 1: $1,000 project Y cash flow exceeds that of project X.

Year 2: $1,212 project X cash flow exceeds that of project Y.

This situation also can be conceived as an investment of $1,000 in year 1 yielding $1,212 in year 2. Such a project W will yield a positive NPV

Exhibit 5.6
Mutually Exclusive Investments: Timing Effects

Project	Initial Outlay	Cash Inflow (End of Year 1)	Cash Inflow (End of Year 2)	NPV at 10%	IRR
X	$2,310	$1,000	$2,000	$251.99	14%
Y	$2,310	$2,000	$ 788	$159.24	16%
W	$ 0	$1,000	$1,212	$101.817	21.19%

of $101.81 and an IRR of 21.19 percent. Thus, project X should be selected. Since the NPV method selected project X, it can again be concluded that the NPV method is preferable.

Live Effects: The Reinvestment Rate Assumption. The NPV and the IRR methods may yield conflicting results when mutually exclusive projects of equal sizes but with different lives are compared. For example, consider the example in Exhibit 5.7, where project X is ranked better with the IRR method, whereas project Y is ranked better with the NPV method. This ranking difference is due to the differences in the investment rate assumption. The IRR method assumes a reinvestment rate equal to the internal rate, whereas the NPV method assumes a reinvestment rate equal to the required rate of return used as a discount factor.

The two reinvestment assumptions can be illustrated by calculating the terminal values of project X under each of the two assumptions. The terminal value using 15 percent for two years is equal to $7,601.50. The terminal value using the required rate of return of 10 percent is equal to $6,957.50. If we compare these two terminal values to the $7,025 terminal value of project Y, we obtain two situations:

1. Using the IRR method, the terminal value of project X, $7,601.50, is greater than the terminal value of project Y, $7,025. The IRR method favors project X.

2. Using the NPV method, the terminal value of project X, $6,957.50, is lower than the terminal value of project Y, $7,025. The NPV method favors project Y.

The assumption of reinvestment at the required rate of return implied in the NPV method is considered to be the better one, the cost of capital being the minimum return acceptable to the firm.

Exhibit 5.7
Mutually Exclusive Investments: Different Lives

Project	Initial Outlay	Cash Inflow			NPV at 10%	IRR
		Year 1	Year 2	Year 3		
X	$5,000	$5,750	–	–	$227.26	15%
Y	$5,000	–	–	$7,025	$277.95	12%

Multiple Internal Rates of Return. Another problem with the IRR method arises from the possibility of multiple IRRs for "abnormal" projects. A "normal" project has one or more outflows followed by a series of inflows. An abnormal project is one that has negative cash flows in periods after the first positive cash flow. With abnormal projects, there may be several different returns which fit the equation, one for each change of the sign of the cash flows.

For example, suppose a capital project requires the following cash flows:

Year	Cash Flow
0	$(1,600)
1	10,000
2	(10,000)

Solving for the IRR, we find two rates: 25 and 400 percent. Neither rate is correct, because neither measures investment value. Instead, the NPV method will give the correct decision and avoid the problem of multiple rates of return associated with some abnormal projects.

PAYBACK METHOD

The payback method, also called the *payout method*, is simply the number of years before the initial cash outlay of a project is fully recovered by its future cash inflows. For example, assume a firm is considering purchasing at $15,000 a delivery truck expected to save $5,000 per year in shipping expenses for four years. The payback formula is

$$\text{Payback} = \frac{\text{Initial cost of the project}}{\text{Annual net cash flows}}$$

$$= \frac{\$15,000}{\$\ 5,000}$$

$$= 3 \text{ years.}$$

In other words, the cost of the delivery truck will be recovered in three years. If the payback period calculated is less than an acceptable maximum payback period, the firm should accept the truck proposal.

For projects with nonuniform cash flows the procedure is slightly different. For example, assume the yearly cash savings are $4,000 in year 1, $5,000 in year 2, $3,000 in year 3, $3,000 in year 4, and $6,000 in year 5. It takes up to year 4 to recover a cumulative cash savings equal to the initial cost of the truck. Therefore, the payback period is four years.

An extension of the payback method is the *bailout method*, which takes into account both the cash savings and the salvage value needed to recover the initial cost of a project. Going back to the first example of the $15,000 truck with an expected savings of $5,000 per year in shipping expenses, assume also that the salvage value is estimated to be $8,000 at the end of year 1 and $5,000 at the end of year 2. The cash savings and salvage value of the truck for the next two years, then, are as follows:

Year	Cash Savings	Salvage Value	Cumulative Cash Savings and Salvage Value
1	$5,000	$8,000	$13,000 = $5,000 + $8,000
2	$5,000	$5,000	$15,000 = $5,000 + $5,000 + $5,000

Thus, at the end of year 2, the total of the cumulative cash savings and the salvage value is equal to the initial cost of the truck. The bailout period is two years.

Businesses commonly use the payback method to provide a quick ranking of capital projects. Some of its features follow, including both advantages and disadvantages:

1. It is easy to calculate and provide a quick answer to the question, How many years will it take before the initial cash outlay is completely recovered?

2. The payback method does not take into account the time value of money. The annual cash flows are given the same weight from one year to another. While the first feature can be interpreted as one of the strengths of the method, this feature is definitely a weakness.

3. The payback method ignores both the cash flows occurring after the payback period and the project's total physical life plan.

4. The payback period can be used to compute the *payback reciprocal*, which is equal to the IRR of the project, providing the project's expected cash flows are constant and are anticipated to continue until infinity. Although projects rarely, if ever, have a perpetual life, a rule of thumb states that the payback reciprocal yields a reasonable approximation of the IRR.[2] The formula for the payback reciprocal is

$$\text{Payback reciprocal} = \frac{r}{\text{Payback period}}.$$

ACCOUNTING RATE OF RETURN METHOD

The ARR method is a capital budgeting evaluation technique that uses the ratio of the average annual profit after taxes to the investment of the project. The ARR formula based on initial investment is

$$\text{ARR} = \frac{\text{Annual revenue from the project} - \text{Annual expense of the project}}{\text{Initial investment}}.$$

The ARR formula based on average investment is

$$\text{ARR} = \frac{\text{Annual revenue from the project} - \text{Annual expenses of the project}}{\text{Average investment}}.$$

These computed ARR values are compared with a cutoff rate before an acceptance or rejection decision is made. For example, assume the Saxon Company is contemplating the purchase of a new machine costing $20,000 and having a five-year useful life and no salvage value. The new machine is expected to generate annual operating revenues of $7,000 and annual expenses of $5,000. The ARR can be computed as follows:

$$\text{ARR based on initial investment:} \frac{\$7,000 - \$5,000}{\$20,000} = 10\%.$$

$$\text{ARR based on average investment} = \frac{\$7,000 - \$5,000}{\frac{\$20,000 + 0}{2}} = 20\%.$$

The ARR then depends on the choice of an initial or average investment base. Using an average investment base leads to substantially higher rates of return. This can be corrected, however, by choosing a higher required cutoff ARR.

The principal strength of the ARR may be its simplicity. It can be computed easily from the accounting records. Since this same characteristic can be perceived as a weakness, the ARR relies on accounting income rather than cash flows. It fails to take into account the timing of cash flows and the time value of money.

METHOD OF CALCULATING DEPRECIATION

The three widely used depreciation methods are the straight-line (SL), sum-of-the-years'-digits (SYD), and double declining balance (DDB) methods. Depreciation charges under the straight-line method are constant over an asset's useful life. Depreciation charges under the latter two methods are higher in the early years of an asset's useful life and taper off rapidly in later years. The best method for tax depreciation maximizes the present value of the depreciation tax shield (that is, reduces income taxes resulting from depreciation expense). The Economic Recovery Act of 1981 introduced new tax lives and an accelerated depreciation method labeled the Accelerated Cost Recovery System (ACRS), which in most cases result in the highest tax shield.

To determine which of the three depreciation methods maximizes the present value of the tax shield, let us use the example of a machine costing $100,000 with a ten-year useful life and no expected salvage value. The required rate of return (r) is 10 percent, and the marginal tax rate (T) is 40 percent.

Straight-Line Depreciation

The annual straight-line depreciation charge is the difference between the cost of an asset (C) and its future salvage value (S) divided by the asset's useful life (N), where t = year:

Annual SL depreciation charge $= SL_t$

$$= \frac{C - S}{N}$$

$$= \frac{\$100,000}{10}$$

$$= \$10,000.$$

$$= \$10,000.$$

Annual SL depreciation rate $= SLR_6$

$$= \frac{SL_t}{C - S}$$

$$= \frac{\$\ 10,000}{100,000} = 10\%$$

Depreciation tax shield $= \sum_{t=1}^{N} \frac{SL_t \times T}{(1 + r)^t}$

$$= \sum_{t=1}^{N} \frac{\$10,000 \times 0.40}{(1 + 0.10)^t}$$

$$= \$24,580.$$

Double Declining Balance Depreciation

Under the DDB method, twice the straight-line rate is applied to the book value of the asset each year until the salvage value is reached:

Annual DDB depreciation $= DDB_t = \dfrac{2}{N} (C - \sum_{i=1}^{t-1} DDB_i).$

Annual DDB rate $= \dfrac{2}{N} = \dfrac{2}{10} = 20\%.$

Depreciation tax shield $= \sum_{t=1}^{n} \dfrac{DDB_t \times T}{(1 + r)^t}.$

Applying these formulas yields the following results:

1 Year	2 Book Value before Depreciation	3 Depreciation	4 Tax Shield (Col. 3 × 40%)	5 Discount Factor at 10%	6 Present Value (Col. 4 × Col. 5)
1	$100,000	$20,000	$8,000	0.909	$ 7,272
2	80,000	16,000	6,400	0.826	5,286
3	64,000	12,800	5,120	0.751	3,845
4	51,200	10,240	4,096	0.683	2,798
5	40,960	8,192	3,277	0.621	2,035
6	32,768	6,554[a]	2,622	0.564	1,479
7	26,214	6,553	2,621	0.513	1,345
8	19,661	6,554	2,622	0.467	1,224
9	13,107	6,553	2,621	0.424	1,111
10	6,554	6,554	2,621	0.386	1,012
Present Value of Tax Shield					$27,407

[a]Under the general guidelines provided in the tax code, firms are permitted to switch from double declining balance to straight-line depreciation when it is to their advantage to do so. They switch at the point that minimizes the tax bill. From the seventh year in this case, SL depreciation charges are higher than DDB charges. This is because we are applying a constant rate to a depreciating balance, which will not carry to the end of the useful life.

Sum-of-the-Years'-Digits Depreciation

Under the SYD method, a mathematical fraction is applied to the base. The numerator for a given year is the number of years remaining in the life of the project taken from the beginning of the year. The denominator is the sum of the series of numbers representing the years of useful life. The sum of the numbers 1 through 10 is equal to 55. N = useful life, t = year, S = salvage value, T = tax rate, and C = acquisition price.

Annual SYD depreciation = SYD_t

$$= (C - S) \frac{N - t}{\frac{N(N + 1)}{2}}$$

$$= (C - S) \frac{2N - t}{\frac{N(N + 1)}{2}}$$

$$\text{Annual SYD rate} = \frac{SYD_t}{C - S}.$$

$$\text{Depreciation tax shield} = \sum_{i=1}^{N} \frac{SYD_t \times T}{(1 + r)^i}.$$

Applying these formulae yields the following results:

1 Year	2 Fraction	3 Depreciation	4 Tax Shield (Col. 3 × 40%)	5 Discount Factor at 10%	6 Present Value (Col. 4 × Col. 5)
1	10/55	$18,182	$7,273	0.909	$ 6,611
2	9/55	16,364	6,546	0.826	5,407
3	8/55	14.545	5,818	0.751	4,369
4	7/55	12,727	5,091	0.683	3,477
5	6/55	10,909	4,364	0.621	2,710
6	5/55	9,091	3,636	0.564	2.051
7	4/55	7,273	2,909	0.513	1,492
8	3/55	5,455	2,182	0.467	1,019
9	2/55	3,636	1,455	0.424	617
10	1/55	1,818	727	0.386	281
Present Value of Tax Shield					$28,033

The present value of the tax shield under each depreciation method has been found to be:

Straight-Line	$24,580
Double Declining Balance	27,407
Sum-of-the-Years'-Digits	28,033

Therefore, the present value of the tax shield is highest under the SYD method for this example, and this method should be used for tax depreciation.

REPLACEMENT DECISIONS

The examples used to illustrate capital budgeting techniques were based on expansion projects. The analysis for replacement projects is slightly different. The following sections illustrate the replacement de-

Exhibit 5.8
Replacement Decision Analysis

Net Outflow at the Time the New Machine is Purchased (t = 0)

	Amount before Taxes	Effect Net of Taxes	Time Even Occurs	PV Factor at 12%	Present Value
1. Cost of New Machine	$30,000	$30,000	0	1.0	$30,000
2. Salvage Value of Old Machine	(4,000)	(4,000)	0	1.0	(4,000)
3. Tax Effect of Sale of Old Machine[a]	(6,000)	(2,880)	0	1.0	(2,880)
4. Investment Tax Credit	(3,000)	(3,000)	0	1.0	(3,000)
5. Total Present Value of Outflows					$20,120

Net Inflows of the Life of the New Machine (t = 1 to 10)

6. Decrease in Operating Costs[b]	$ 6,000	$ 3,120	1 to 10	5.650	$17,628
7. Depreciation on New Machine	2,400	–	–	–	–
8. Depreciation on Old Machine	1,000	–	–	–	–
9. Net Changes in Tax Savings from Depreciation	1,400	672	1 to 10	5.650	3,797
10. Salvage Value of New Machine	$ 6,000	$ 6,000	1 to 10	0.322	1,932
11. Total Present Value of Inflows					$23,357
12. NPV = $23,357 – $20,120 = $3,237					

[a]The tax effect of sale of old machine = Loss × t = [($10,000 – $4,000) × 0.48] = $2,880.

[b]Cost reduction = Decrease in cost × (1 – t) = $4,000 (1 – 0.48) = $2,080.

cision first where the lives of the project are equal, and second where the lives of the project are unequal.

Replacement Decisions: Equal Lives

Assume that a machine purchased ten years ago by the Litton Company at a cost of $20,000 had an expected 20-year life when purchased and zero salvage value. A straight-line depreciation charge of $2,000 makes the machine's present book value equal to $10,000. A new machine now being considered to replace the old one can be purchased for $30,000 and is expected to reduce operating costs from $10,000 to $4,000 for its ten-year useful life. The old machine can be sold for $4,000. The new machine is expected to have a $6,000 salvage value. Taxes are 48 percent, and an investment tax credit of 10 percent of the purchase price can be claimed on the purchase of the new machine.[3] The cost of capital is 12 percent. Should the Litton Company replace the old machine?

The NPV of the replacement decision, computed in Exhibit 5.8, is

$3,237. The new machine should be purchased to replace the old machine, given that it increases the value to the firm by $3,237.

Replacement Decisions: Unequal Lives

The procedure generally used to choose between two mutually exclusive replacement proposals with unequal lives is to convert the number of years of analysis to a common termination year through a series of *replacement chains*. For example, to choose between a four-year project X and a six-year project Y, it is necessary to compare a three-chain cycle for project X and a two-chain cycle for project Y, bringing the common termination year to 12.

Assume that the Shields Company is considering replacing a fully depreciated machine with one of two replacement machines. Machine X has a cost of $15,000, a five-year useful life, and will generate after-tax cash flows of $5,000 per year for five years. Machine Y has a cost of $18,000, a ten-year useful life, and will generate after-tax cash flows of $4,000 per year for ten years. The company's cost of capital is 12 percent.

To determine which machine should be chosen, the NPV of each machine can be computed:

$$NPV\ (X) = \$5,000(3.605) - \$15,000 = \$3,025.$$
$$NPV\ (Y) = \$4,000(5.605) - \$18,000 = \$4,600.$$

From these computations it appears that machine Y should be chosen. The analysis is incorrect, however, since a second investment can be made after five years if machine X is chosen, and the second investment may be profitable. A better analysis would be based on the common denominator of ten years. Therefore,

	Present value of first investment of machine X	+	Present value of second investment of machine Y
$NPV\ (X) =$			
	$= \$3,025 + \$3,025(0.567)$		$= \$4,740.$
$NPV\ (Y) =$			$= \$4,600.$

The NPV of machine X is $4,740, which is higher than the NPV of machine Y.

CAPITAL RATIONING

Capital rationing exists when a firm faces limited supplies of funds, which precludes the acceptance of potentially profitable projects. Among the causes cited for capital rationing are (1) limits imposed on new borrowing, (2) a debt limit imposed by an outside agreement (for example, bond covenants), (3) limits on capital spending imposed on divisional management, and (4) management's desire to maintain a given dividend policy or a specific earnings per share or price/earnings ratio.[4]

Conventional methods of evaluation with capital rationing consist of (1) ranking the projects under consideration from highest to lowest for whichever evaluation model is used—that is, IRR, NPV, or PI; and (2) selecting projects starting at the top of the ranking until funds are exhausted. Although these conventional methods based on either the IRR or the NPV techniques are simple, discontinuities or size disparities between projects prevent the choice of optimal projects. For example, a 20 percent return on $1,000 is considered better than a 15 percent return on $2,000, according to the conventional capital rationing method.

To correct the limitations of the conventional capital rationing methods, mathematical programming can be used to select the optimal combination of projects. In 1955, James H. Lorie and Leonard J. Savage were the first to suggest mathematical programming—in the form of a heuristic programming approach—to deal with capital rationing.[5] This attempt was followed by a more comprehensive treatment of the problem by H. Martin Weingartner, whose basic model follows:[6]

Maximize

$$\sum_{j=1}^{m} b_j X_j,$$

Subject to

$$\sum_{j=1}^{m} C_{ij} X_j \le C_t \text{ for } t = 1, \ldots, n.$$

$$0 \le X_j \le 1.$$

X_j is an integer,

where

Exhibit 5.9
Capital Rationing Example

Investment Proposal	Present Value of Outlay (Period 1)	Present Value of Outlay (Period 2)	NPV
1	$10	$ 5	$20
2	20	10	30
3	30	10	40
4	40	30	50

b_j = Net present value of investment proposal j.

X_j = 0 if the project is accepted, and 1 if the project is rejected.

C_{tj} = Net cash needed for proposal j in period t.

C_t = Total budget for period t.

Because of the use of the last two constraints, this mathematical programming model is known as *integer programming*.

To illustrate the integer programming approach to capital budgeting, let us use the data shown in Exhibit 5.9. The present values of the two budget constraints are $90 in period 1 and $30 in period 2. The model will look like the following:

Maximize

$$20x_1 + 30x_2 + 40x_3 + 50x_4,$$

Subject to

$$10x_1 + 20x_2 + 30x_3 + 40x_4 \leq 90.$$

$$5x_1 + 10x_2 + 10x_3 + 30x_4 \leq 30.$$

$$0 \leq X_j \leq 1 \text{ for } j = 1, 2, 3, \text{ and } 4.$$

X_j is an integer.

CAPITAL BUDGETING UNDER UNCERTAINTY

Nature of Risk

Because the cash of a project often may be estimated on the basis of incomplete information, the capital budgeting evaluation must be performed in a climate of uncertainty. Although *uncertainty* and *risk* are sometimes used synonymously, they are different in the strict mathematical sense. *Risk* refers to the possible outcomes of a project to which probabilities can be assigned, whereas *uncertainty* refers to outcomes to which it is difficult to assign probabilities. Thus, the real interest lies with risk, because it is measurable.

Most decision makers are risk averse and perceive risk in different ways:

1. The *dollar price* risk is the risk associated with a decline in the number of dollars used to acquire a financial asset.
2. The *purchasing power* risk is the risk associated with a decline in the purchasing power of the monetary unit.
3. The *interest rate* risk is the risk associated with changes in the interest rate, which affect market values of many types of securities.
4. The *business risk* is the risk associated with the operational cash flows of a firm.
5. The *financial risk* is the risk associated with financial leverage.
6. The *systematic risk* or *market risk* is the risk associated with the common stocks of a particular industry.
7. The *unsystematic risk* is the risk associated with a particular company.

Because the perception of risk by decision makers affects their decisions, it should be taken into account in the decision making process. Capital budgeting under uncertainty should incorporate risk in the evaluation process.

Risk-Adjusted Discount Rate Method

One of the techniques for incorporating risk in the evaluation process is the risk-adjusted discount rate, which consists of manipulating the discount rate applied to the cash flows to reflect the amount of risk inherent in a project. The higher the risk associated with a project, the higher the discount rate applied to the cash flows. If a given project is perceived to be twice as risky as most acceptable projects to the firm and the cost of capital is 12 percent, then the correct risk-adjusted discount rate is 24 percent.

In spite of the simplicity, the risk-adjusted discount rate method is subject to the following limitations:

1. The determination of the exact risk-adjusted discount rate is subjective and, therefore, subject to error.
2. The method adjusts the discount rate rather than the future cash flows, which are subject to variability and risk.

Certainty Equivalent Method

Another technique for incorporating in the evaluation process is the certainty equivalent method, which involves adjusting the future cash flows so a project can be evaluated on a riskless basis. The adjustment is formulated as follows:

$$NPV = \sum_{t=1}^{n} \left[\frac{\alpha_t CF_t}{(1 + R_F)} \right] - I_0,$$

where

α_t = Risk coefficient applied to the cash flow of period t (CF_t).
I_0 = Initial cost of the project.
R_F = Risk-free rate.

As the formula shows, the method proceeds by multiplying the future cash flows by certainty equivalents to obtain a riskless cash flow. Note also that the discount rate used is R_F, which is a risk-free rate of interest.

To illustrate the certainty equivalent method, assume an investment with the following characteristics:

I_0 = Initial cost = $30,000.
CF_1 = Cash flow, year 1 = $10,000.
CF_2 = Cash flow, year 2 = $20,000.
CF_3 = Cash flow, year 3 = $30,000.
α_1 = Certainty equivalent, year 1 = 0.9.
α_2 = Certainty equivalent, year 2 = 0.8.
α_3 = Certainty equivalent, year 3 = 0.6.

The NPV of the investment using a risk-free discount rate of 6 percent is computed as follows:

Period	Cash Flow (CF,)	Risk Coefficient (a,)	Certainty Equivalent	Risk-free Rate (R_F)	Present Value
1	$10,000	0.9	$ 9,000	0.943	$ 8,487
2	20,000	0.8	16,000	0.890	14,240
3	30,000	0.6	18,000	0.840	15,120
Present Value of Cash Flows					$37,847
Initial Investment					30,000
Net Present Value					$ 7,847

Since the NPV is positive, the investment should be considered acceptable. The main advantage of the certainty equivalent is that it allows the assignment of a different risk factor to each cash flow, given that a risk can concentrate in one or more periods.

The certainty equivalent method and a risk-adjusted discount rate method are comparable methods of evaluating risk. To produce similar ranking, the following equation must hold:

$$\frac{\alpha_t \, CF_t}{(1 + R_F)^t} = \frac{CF_t}{(1 + R_A)^t}.$$

where

α_t = Risk coefficient used in the certainty equivalent method.

R_F = Risk-free discount rate.

R_A = Risk-adjusted discount rate used in the risk-adjusted discount rate method.

CF_t = Future cash flow.

Solving for α_t yields

$$\alpha_t = \frac{(1 + R_F)^t}{(1 + R_A)^t}$$

Given that R_A and R_F are constant and $R_A > R_F$, and α_t decreases over time, this means that risk increases over time. To illustrate, assume that in the previous example $R_A = 15\%$. Then

$$\alpha_1 = \frac{(1 + R_F)^1}{(1 + R_A)^1} = \frac{(1 + 0.06)^1}{(1 + 0.15)^1} = 0.921.$$

$$\alpha_2 = \frac{(1 + R_F)^2}{(1 + R_A)^2} = \frac{(1 + 0.06)^2}{(1 + 0.15)^2} = 0.848.$$

$$\alpha_3 = \frac{(1 + R_F)^3}{(1 + R_A)^3} = \frac{(1 + 0.06)^3}{(1 + 0.15)^3} = 0.783.$$

In many cases this assumption of increasing risk may not be realistic.

Probability Distribution

The probability distribution approach to the evaluation of risk assigns probabilities to each cash flow outcome. Various measures of risk then can be computed, giving information about the dispersion or tightness of the probability distribution. *Standard deviation* is a conventional measure of dispersion. For a single period, the standard deviation is computed as follows:

$$\sigma_1 = \sqrt{\sum_{i=1}^{n} [X_{it} - E_t(X)]^2\, P(X_i)_t,}$$

where

σ_t = Standard deviation of period t's cash flow.
X_{it} = Cash flow for the ith outcome in period t.
$E_t(X)$ = Expected value of cash flow in period t.
$P(X_i)$ = Probability of occurrence of cash flow X_i in period t.

The expected cash flow $E_t(X)$ is computed as follows:

$$E_t(X) = \sum_{i=1}^{n} X_{it} P(X)_{t},$$

All things being equal, the higher the standard deviation, the greater the risk associated with the expected value.

Another measure of relative dispersion is the *coefficient of variation* (CV), a measure that compares the expected value and risk of probability distribution. The coefficient of variation is computed as follows:

$$CV = \frac{\sigma}{E(X)}.$$

All things being equal, the smaller the coefficient of variation, the better the project. To illustrate these risk concepts, assume that projects A and B have the following discrete probability distributions of expected cash flows in each of the next three years:

Project A		**Project B**	
Probability	*Cash Flow*	*Probability*	*Cash Flow*
0.2	$1,000	0.3	$1,500
0.5	2,000	0.3	1,000
0.2	3,000	0.2	3,500
0.1	4,000	0.2	3,750

The expected value of cash flows of both projects can be computed as follows:

$$E(A) = 0.2(\$1,000) + 0.5(\$2,000) + 0.2(\$3,000) + 0.1(\$4,000) = \$2,200.$$
$$E(B) = 0.3(\$1,500) + 0.3(\$1,000) + 0.2(\$3,500) + 0.2(\$3,750) = \$2,200.$$

On the basis of expected values as a measure of central tendency in the distribution, projects A and B are equivalent. To determine which project is riskier, the standard deviations for both projects can be computed as follows:

$$\sigma(A) = [0.2(\$1,000 - \$2,000)^2 + 0.5(\$2,000 - \$2,200)^2 + 0.2(\$3,000 - \$2,200)^2 + 0.1(\$4,000 - \$2,200)^2]^{\frac{1}{2}} = \$871.77.$$

$$\sigma(B) = [0.3(\$1,500 - \$2,200)^2 + 0.3(\$1,000 - \$2,200)^2 + 0.2(\$3,500 - \$2,200) + 0.2(\$3,750 - \$2,200)^2]^{\frac{1}{2}} = \$1,182.15.$$

Thus, project B has a significantly higher standard deviation, indicating a greater dispersion of possible cash flows.

The standard deviation is an absolute measure of risk. For comparison, the projects should also be evaluated on the basis of their coefficient of variation, which measures the relative dispersion within the distribution. The coefficient of variation for both projects can be computed now:

$$CV(A) = \frac{\sigma_A}{E(A)} \times 100 = \frac{\$871.77}{\$2,200} = 39.6\%.$$

$$CV(B) = \frac{\sigma_B}{E(B)} \times 100 = \frac{\$1,182.15}{\$2,200} = 53.7\%.$$

The coefficient of variation for project B is significantly higher than for project A, which indicates again that project B presents a greater degree of risk.

The coefficient of variation is an especially useful measure when the comparison between projects leads to the acceptance of a given project based on a comparison between means, or when the comparison leads to the acceptance of a different project based on a comparison between standard deviations.

Multiperiod Projects

The computation of the measures of risk becomes more complicated when several periods are involved. Some assumptions must be made regarding the relationships between the period cash flows—namely, whether the cash flows are dependent or independent.

To illustrate, let us return to project A and assume (1) that the applicable discount rate (R) is 10 percent and (2) that the project calls for a $5,000 investment. Independent of the nature of the relationship between cash flows in the three periods, the NPV of project A can be computed as follows:

$$NPV = \sum_{i=1}^{3}\left[\frac{\$2,200}{(1 + 0.10)^i}\right] - \$5,000 = \$471.$$

The standard deviation of the project will be computed as differently according to whether we assume that the cash flows are dependent, independent, or mixed.

Independent Cash Flows

If we assume serial independence of the cash flows between the periods, the standard deviation of the entire project is

$$\sigma = \sqrt{\sum_{i=1}^{n}\frac{\sigma_t^2}{(1 + r)^{2t}}},$$

where

σ_t = standard deviation of the probability distribution of the cash flows in period t.

Hence the standard deviation of project A, assuming serial independence, is

$$\sigma_A = \sqrt{\frac{(\$871)^2}{(1 + 0.10)^2} + \frac{(\$871)^2}{(1 + 0.10)^4} + \frac{(\$871)^2}{(1 + 0.10)^6}} = \$358.04.$$

Dependent Cash Flows

In general, the cash flows of a given period are expected to influence the cash flows of subsequent periods. In the case of perfect correlation, the standard deviation of the entire project is

$$\sigma = \sum_{i=1}^{n} \frac{\sigma_t}{(1 + r)^t} .$$

Therefore, the standard deviation of project A, assuming perfect correlation between interperiod cash flows, is

$$\sigma_A = \sum_{i=1}^{3} \frac{\$871}{(1 + 0.10)^i} = \$2,166.17.$$

Note that the standard deviation under the assumption of independence is $358.04, while under the assumption of perfect dependency it is considerably higher ($2,166.17). If the cash flows are perfectly correlated there is more risk inherent in the project than if the cash flows are independent.

Mixed Correlation

A project may include some independent and some dependent cash flows. Frederick Hillier proposed a model to deal with a mixed situation:[7]

$$\sigma = \sum_{t=0}^{T} \frac{\sigma^Y_{2t}}{(1 + r)^{2t}} + \sum_{j=1}^{m} \left[\sum_{j=1}^{T} \frac{6_{zjt}}{(1 + r)t} \right]^2,$$

where

Y_t = The independent component of the net cash flow in period t.

Z_{jt} = The jth perfectly correlated component of the net cash flow in period t.

To illustrate the computation of the standard deviation of a project with mixed correlation, Hillier assumed the following project data for a new product addition:

Year	Source	Expected Value of Net Cash Flows (In Thousands)	Standard Deviation
0	Initial Investment	$(600)	$ 50
1	Production Cash Outflow	(250)	20
2	Production Cash Outflow	(200)	10
3	Production Cash Outflow	(200)	10
4	Production Cash Outflow	(200)	10
5	Prod. Outflow-Salvage Value	(100)	$10\sqrt{10}$
1	Marketing	300	50
2	Marketing	600	100
3	Marketing	500	100
4	Marketing	400	100
5	Marketing	300	100

Hillier also assumed that all the outflows were independent and that all marketing flows were perfectly correlated. If 10 percent is used at the risk-free rate, the expected value of the NPV for the proposal is

$$NPV = \sum_{t=1}^{S} \left[\frac{X}{(1 + 0.10)^t} \right] - C_0$$

or

$$NPV = \frac{\$300 - \$250}{(1.10)} + \frac{\$600 - \$200}{(1.10)^2} + \frac{\$500 - \$200}{(1.10)^3}$$
$$+ \frac{\$400 - \$200}{(1.10)^4} + \frac{\$300 - \$100}{(1.10)^5} - \$600 = \$262.$$

The standard deviation is

$$\sigma = \sqrt{50^2 + \frac{20^2}{(1.10)^2} + \ldots + \frac{(10\sqrt{10})^2}{(1.10)^{10}} + \left[\frac{50}{(1.10)} + \ldots + \frac{100}{(1.10)^5} \right]^2} = \$339.$$

Exhibit 5.10
Decision Tree Approach to Capital Budgeting

Period 1		Period 2				Total	Expected Value of Total
Net Cash Flows A_1	Initial Probability $p(1)$	Net Cash Flows A_2	Conditional Probability $p(2/1)$	Number of Cases	Joint Probability[a] p_j	Net Cash Flows[b] A_j	Net Cash Flows
		$20	0.3	1	0.18	$50	$ 9.00
	0.6	30	0.4	2	0.24	60	14.40
$30		40	0.3	3	0.18	70	12.60
		30	0.2	4	0.08	70	5.60
40	0.4	40	0.5	5	0.2	80	16.00
		50	0.3	6	0.12	90	10.80
Mean Value							$68.40

[a]$p_j = p(1) \times p(2/1)$.

[b]$A_1 + A_2$.

Moderate Correlation

In most cases, cash flows cannot be easily classified as either independent or perfectly correlated, and a decision tree approach can be used. In a capital budgeting context, this approach involves the multiplication of the conditional probabilities of correlated periods to obtain the joint probabilities that will specify the probabilities of multiple events. Exhibit 5.10 illustrates the decision tree approach to compute the joint probabilities and the expected value of a project.

Simulation

The preceding methods of dealing with uncertainty apply only when two probability distributions are considered. In most realistic capital budgeting situations, more than two variables are significant, and more than two variables are subject to uncertainty. The simulation technique takes into account the interacting variables and their corresponding probability distributions. David B. Hertz proposed a simulation model to obtain the dispersion about the expected rate of return for an investment proposal.[8] He established nine separate probability distributions to determine the probability distribution of the average rate of return for the entire project. The following nine variables are considered.

Market analysis:

1. Market size
2. Selling price
3. Market growth rate
4. Share of market

Investment cost analysis:

5. Investment required
6. Residual value of investment

Operating and fixed costs:

7. Operating costs
8. Fixed costs
9. Useful life of facilities

The computer simulates trial values of each of the nine variables and then computes the return on investment based on the simulated values obtained. These trials are repeated often enough to obtain a frequency distribution for the return on the investment. This approach can also be used to determine the NPV or the IRR of a project.

CAPITAL BUDGETING UNDER INFLATION

Beginning with seminal work by Irving Fisher, economists have shown fairly conclusively that market rates of interest include an adjustment of expected inflation rate—the nonexistent "homogeneous expectation." This consensus forecast, therefore, is built into the discount rate used in capital budgeting. When rates of inflation were relatively low (say 2 to 3 percent), this did not lead to serious distortions in the IRR or NPV models, because any error in the rate estimation was immaterial in most cases. With the higher rates of inflation we are now experiencing, it is desirable to explicitly consider the rate of inflation in developing cash flow forecasts. The correct analysis can be done in either of two ways: (1) using a money discount rate to discount money cash flows, or (2) using a real discount rate to discount real cash flows.

Before illustrating either approach, let us explore the differences between money cash flows and real cash flows, and between real discount rate and money discount rate. Money cash flows are cash flows measured in dollars from various periods having different purchasing power. Real cash flows are cash flows measured in dollars having the same purchasing power. The real cash flow given for a given year, expressed in terms of dollars of $year_0$ (the base year) is equal to the money cash flow for that year, multiplied by the following ratio:

$$\frac{\text{Price level index in } year_0}{\text{Price level index in } year_t}$$

For example, if an investment promises a money return of $100 for three years and the price index for years 0 through 3 is 100, 110, 121, and 133.1, respectively, then the real cash flows are as follows:

Year 1: $100 × 100/110   = 90.90.
Year 2: $100 × 100/121   = 82.64.
Year 3: $100 × 100/133.1 = 75.13.

The money discount rate, r, can also be computed. Assuming that f is the annual rate of inflation, i is the real discount rate, and the decision maker is in the zero tax bracket, then

$$r = (1 + f)(1 + i) - 1,$$

or

$$r = i + f + if.$$

For example, if the real return before taxes is 3 percent, and the rate of inflation is 10 percent, then the nominal discount rate is

$$0.03 + 0.10 + 0.003 = 0.133.$$

To illustrate the correct analysis under inflation, assume the same data as in the previous example. The correct analysis can be either of two, as follows:

1. The first analysis discounts the money cash flows using a money discount rate. The present value of the investment will be computed as follows:

Period	Money Cash Flow	Nominal Present Value Factor at 13.3%	Present Value
1	100	0.8826	88.26
2	100	0.7792	77.92
3	100	0.6874	68.74
			234.92

2. The second analysis discounts the real cash flows using a real discount rate. The present value of the investment will give the same present value, as follows:

Period	Real Cash Flow	Real Present Value at 3%	Present Value
1	90.90	0.9709	88.254
2	82.64	0.9426	77.896
3	75.13	0.9151	68.751
			234.901

Assuming a marginal tax rate t on nominal income, the nominal discount rate will be computed as follows:

$$1 + (1 - t)r + (1 + f) + 1 + i(1 - t),$$

or

$$r = i + if + f/(1 - t).$$

Assuming the tax rate to be 30 percent, the nominal rate is then computed as follows:

$$r = 0.03 + (0.03 \times 0.10) + 0.10/ (1 - 0.30)$$
$$= 0.1758.$$

In other words, a nominal rate of 17.58 percent is needed for an investor in a 30 percent tax bracket and facing an inflation rate of 10 percent to earn a real discount rate of 3 percent.

CONCLUSION

Many capital budgeting techniques exist in the literature and the practice. The discounted cash flow methods take the time value of money into account to evaluate capital budgeting proposals. The two basic discounted cash flow methods are the internal rate of return and the net present value methods. Management should consider some of the conflicts between these two methods when choosing between them. Other problems in using capital budgeting techniques include problems with replacement decisions, problems with capital rationing, and problems with capital budgeting under certainty.

NOTES

1. Ahmed Belkaoui, *Conceptual Foundations of Management Accounting* (Reading, Mass.: Addison-Wesley, 1980,) pp. 58–60.

2. The exact rule, introduced by M. J. Gordon in 1995, states that provided the economic life of a project is equal to or greater than twice the payback period, the payback reciprocal yields a reasonable approximation of the project's IRR. Gordon also mentioned that if a project's life exceeds twice the payback period by two or three years (for projects with payoffs of no more than five years), the payback reciprocal will be incorrect by approximately 10 percent.

3. This means that 10 percent of the investment cost can be deducted directly from taxes due in the years of the investment.

4. James M. Fremgen, "Capital Budgeting Practices: A Survey," *Management Accounting* (May 1973), pp. 23–24.

5. James H. Lorie and Leonard J. Savage, "Three Problems in Rationing Capital," *Journal of Business* (October 1955), pp. 229–239.

6. H. Martin Weingartner, *Mathematical Programming and the Analysis of Capital Budgeting Problems* (Englewood Cliffs, N.J.: Prentice-Hall, 1963).

7. Frederick Hillier, "The Deviation of Probabilistic Information for the Evaluation of Risky Investments," *Management Science* (April 1963), pp. 443–457.

8. David B. Hertz, "Risk Analysis in Capital Investment," *Harvard Business Review* (January–February 1964), pp. 95–106; and David B. Hertz, "Investment Policies Pay Off," *Harvard Business Review* (January–February 1968), pp. 96–108.

SELECTED READINGS

Bailes, Jack C., James F. Nielsen, and Steve Wendell. "Capital Budgeting in the Forest Products Industry." *Management Accounting* (July 1979), pp. 46–51, 57.

Bavishi, Vinod B. "Capital Budgeting Practices at Multinationals." *Management Accounting* (August 1981), pp. 32–35.

Bergeron, Pierre G. "The Other Dimensions of the Payback Period." *Cost and Management* (May–June 1978), pp. 35–39.

Doenges, R. Conrad. "The Reinvestment Problem in a Practical Perspective." *Financial Management* (Spring 1972), pp. 85–91.

Elliot, Grover S. "Analysis of the Cost of Capital." *Management Accounting* (December 1980), pp. 13–18.

Fremgen, James M. "Capital Budgeting Practices: A Survey." *Management Accounting* (May 1973), pp. 19–25.

Gaertner, James F. and Ken Milani. "The TRR Yardstick for Hospital Capital Expenditure Decisions." *Management Accounting* (December 1980), pp. 25–33.

Glahn, Gerald L., Kent T. Fields, and Jerry E. Trapnell. "How to Evaluate Mixed Risk Capital Projects." *Management Accounting* (December 1980), pp. 34–38.

Hendricks, James A. "Capital Budgeting Decisions: NPV or IRR?" *Cost and Management* (March–April 1980), pp. 16–20.

Hertz, David B. "Investment Policies That Pay Off." *Harvard Business Review* (January–February 1968), pp. 96–108.

Hertz, David B. "Risk Analysis in Capital Investment." *Harvard Business Review* (January–February 1964), pp. 95–106.

Hespos, Richard F. and Paul A. Strassman. "Stochastic Decision Trees for the Analysis of Investment Decisions." *Management Science* (August 1965), pp. 244–259.

Hillier, Frederick. "The Deviation of Probabilistic Information for the Evaluation of Risky Investment." *Management Science* (April 1963), pp. 443–457.

Hing-Ling, Amy and Hong-Shiang Lau. "Improving Present Value Analysis with a Programmable Calculator." *Management Accounting* (November 1979), pp. 52–57.

Johnson, Robert W. *Capital Budgeting* (Belmont, Calif.: Wadsworth Publishing, 1970).

Kim, Suk H. "Making the Long-term Investment Decision." *Management Accounting* (March 1979), pp. 41–49.

Kim, Suk H. and Edward J. Farragher. "Current Capital Budgeting Practices." *Management Accounting* (June 1981), pp. 26–31.

Lerner, Eugene M. and Alfred Rappaport. "Limit DCF in Capital Budgeting." *Harvard Business Review* (September–October 1968), pp. 133–139.

Norgaard, Corine T. "The Post-Completion Audit of Capital Projects." *Cost and Management* (January–February 1979), pp. 19–25.

Osteryoung, Jerome S. *Capital Budgeting: Long-Term Asset Selection* (Columbus, Ohio: Grid, 1974).

Osteryoung, Jerome S., Elton Scott, and Gordon S. Roberts. "Selecting Capital Projects with the Coefficient of Variation." *Financial Management* (Summer 1977), pp. 65–70.

Pettway, Richard H. "Integer Programming in Capital Budgeting: A Note on Computational Experience." *Journal of Financial and Quantitative Analysis* (September 1973), pp. 655–672.

Puglisi, D. J. and L. W. Chadwick. "Capital Budgeting with Realized Terminal Values." *Cost and Management* (May–June 1977), pp. 13–17.

Raiborn, D. D. and Thomas A. Ratcliffe. "Are You Accounting for Inflation in Your Capital Budgeting Process?" *Management Accounting* (September 1979), pp. 19–22.

Roemmich, Roger A., Gordon L. Duke, and William H. Gates. "Maximizing the Present Value of Tax Savings from Depreciation." *Management Accounting* (September 1978), pp. 55–57, 63.

Sangeladji, Mohammad A. "True Rate of Return for Evaluating Capital Investments." *Management Accounting* (February 1979), pp. 24–27.

Suver, James D. and Bruce R. Neumann. "Capital Budgeting for Hospitals." *Management Accounting* (December 1978), pp. 48–50, 53.

Truitt, Jack F. "A Solution to Capital Budgeting Problems Concerning Investments with Different Lives." *Cost and Management* (November–December 1978), pp. 44–45.

Uhl, Franklin S. "Automated Capital Investment Decisions." *Management Accounting* (April 1980), pp. 41–46.

Weingartner, H. Martin. "Capital Budgeting of Interrelated Projects: Surveys and Synthesis." *Management Science* (March 1966), pp. 485–516.

William, H. Jean. "On Multiple Rates of Return." *Journal of Finance* (March 1968), pp. 187–191.

Index

Accelerated Cost Recovery System (ACRS), 119
Alternative minimum tax (AMT) rules, 40
Annual reports, noncancelable operating lease commitments in, 84

Bethlehem Steel Corporation, 8

Capital budgeting: administration of, 100; estimation of relevant cash flows in, 101–4; evaluation of, 99
Capital lease: constructive capitalization and, 84–87; criteria, 41; decision, 39–40; financial statement effects of SFAS No. 13 and, 88–90; key elements of, 42–43; lessee accounting in, 42–47; minimum lease payments in, 42
Capital project evaluation: accounting rate of return method in, 118–19; certainty equivalent method in, 128–30; discounted cash flow methods in, 104–16; inflation and, 136–38; in multiperiod projects, 132–36; net present value computation in, 112–16; payback method in, 116–18; perceptions of risk in, 126–27; probability distribution approach in, 130–32; for replacement,

122–24; risk-adjusted discount rate method in, 127–28
Capital rationing, 125–26
Car leasing, open-end lease in, 4
Cash borrowing capacity, buy-or-lease decision and, 5
Change in present value approach (CPV), 82–84

Debt financing: versus lease financing, 6; restrictions, 5
Depreciation: double declining balance, 120–21; straight-line, 119–20; sum-of-years'-digits, 121–22
Direct financing lease, 42; lessor accounting for, 47–51
Direct leasing, 3
Discount rate calculations, 15–18

Economic Recovery Tax Act of 1981, transfer of tax benefits and, 7–8

Financial Accounting Standards Board (FASB): definition of lease, 39; Statement No. 13, 39, 41, 82, 88
Financial lease, versus operating lease, 2
Financial statement, lease capitalization rules and, 88

Financing decision. *See* Lease-or-buy analysis
Ford Motor Company, 8

Initial direct costs, accounting treatment for, 63
International Business Machines Corporation (IBM), 8
Investment decision, internal rate of return computation in, 19, 104–16. *See also* Lease-or-buy analysis

Lease/leasing: balance sheet advantages of, 40; benefits for lessee, 4–8, 40; benefits for lessor, 47; leveraged, 3, 66–67; motivations for, 24–25; types of, 2–4
Lease accounting: for capital lease by lessee; capitalization versus expensing in, 81, 87–88, 90–94; constructive capitalization in, 84–87; current portion of long-term obligation in, 82–84; of guaranteed residual value, 53–56; for initial direct costs by lessor, 63; for lessor in, 47–51; for leveraged leases, 67–79; net present value advantage of leasing (NAL) in, 10; for real estate leases, 65–66; regulations, 81–82; of residual value, 53–56; rules, 81–82; of sale-leaseback, 63–65; of sales-type lease for lessor, 60–62; of unguaranteed residual value, 56–60
Lease disclosure rule: economic consequences of, 87–94; financial ratios based on, 94–95; financial statement effects of, 88–90
Lease-or-buy analysis: calculation methods in, 25–26; decision format, 22–24; Johnson and Lewellen model of, 14–18; lessor's rental payment computation in, 9–10; mix of assets and, 6; normative model for, 33–36; Roenfeldt and Osteryoung model of, 18–21; tax benefits in, 6–8, 47. *See also* Capital project evaluation

Long-term obligations, measure of current portion of, 82–84

Maintenance lease, 4
McDonald's Corporation, 84–87

Net lease, 4
Nonmaintenance lease, 4

Operating expenses, rental payments as, 6
Operating lease: accounting, 46–47; balance sheet/annual reports and, 84; criteria, 41, 42; versus financial lease, 2
Ownership risks, 4

Personal property leases, types of, 41–42

R. R. Donnelley & Sons Co., 8
Real estate lease accounting, 65–66
Rental payments: lessor's computation of, 9–10; as operating expenses, 6
Residual value: as benefit of leasing, 47; guaranteed, 42; lease payment computation and, 53–56; lessor and, 58–60; unguaranteed, 56–58

Safe-harbor leasing, 7–8
Sale-leaseback arrangement: accounting for, 63–65; versus direct lease, 3; transfer of tax benefits and, 8
Sales-type lease, 41; versus direct financing lease, 60; lessor accounting in, 60–62
Stockholders' wealth maximization model, 99

Tax incentives/shelters, 3, 47; depreciation methods and, 119–22; in lease-or-buy decision, 6–8, 29–32; leveraged lease and, 66

About the Author

AHMED RIAHI-BELKAOUI is CBA Distinguished Professor of Accounting in the College of Business Administration, University of Illinois at Chicago. Author of more than 30 Quorum books and coauthor of several more, he is also a prolific author of articles published in the major scholarly and professional journals of his field, and has served on numerous editorial boards that oversee them.

ISBN 1-56720-147-4

EAN

9 781567 201475

HARDCOVER BAR CODE